MW00461165

THE BOY AND THE MOUNTAIN

PRAISE FOR *IN PRAISE OF PATHS*

"What [Ekelund]'s addressing is the intention to walk one's way to meaning: the walk as spiritual exercise, a kind of vision quest in which the answers we arrive at are less important than the impulse to seek them."

THE NEW YORK TIMES

"A charming read, celebrating the relationship between humans and their bodies, their landscapes, and one another."

THE WASHINGTON POST

"This lovely book taps into something primeval in us all."

STAR TRIBUNE

"[R]ethinking the social, historical, and spiritual needs that are met by putting one foot in front of the other."

OUTSIDE MAGAZINE

"[Urges] a return to our ambulatory origins . . . [N]ever low on zeal."

THE WALL STREET JOURNAL

"[Ekelund] invites his readers to join him on his chosen path, a path that involves regular walking with careful mindfulness. This is an invitation we should all accept."

VANCOUVER SUN

"A deeply fascinating meditation on the paths we take through our environment and our lives."

ERLING KAGGE, author of *Silence: In the Age of Noise* and *Walking: One Step at a Time*

"A quiet, reflective read."

BOOKLIST

"An easygoing, gently unfolding memoir, it soothes in difficult times."

THE FREE PRESS (WINNIPEG)

PRAISE FOR *A YEAR IN THE WOODS*

"A funny and relatable story of a city man trying to find some life balance. Ekelund is a new, much-needed model of the Norwegian explorer, perfect for our times."
FLORENCE WILLIAMS, author of *The Nature Fix: Why Nature Makes Us Happier, Healthier, and More Creative*

"A topical and beguiling book. Admirably humble and honest."
TRISTAN GOOLEY, author of *The Natural Navigator*

"Calm and charming ... [this] book leaves the reader with the pleasant sense of meeting a new and civilized friend who tells good stories."
VANCOUVER SUN

"A lovely little book."
TORONTO STAR

"A wonderful reminder of the importance of meandering without a goal and that as nature moves by all we seek is equilibrium. Sit by the campfire and smell the wood and the smoke and let Torbjørn show you how."
MARC HAMER, author of *Seed to Dust* and *How to Catch a Mole*

"This determination to live his life deliberately, to pay attention to the natural world, is inspiring, as is his philosophy that meaning can come from small gestures."
STAR TRIBUNE

"With all the turbulence and chaos of recent times, so many of us are yearning for our own small journeys into nature. The world needs more of this, and more stories such as *A Year in the Woods*."
ALASTAIR HUMPHREYS, author of *Microadventures: Local Discoveries for Great Escapes*

TORBJØRN EKELUND

TRANSLATED BY BECKY L. CROOK

THE
BOY

AND THE
MOUNTAIN

A Father, His Son, and a
Journey of Discovery

GREYSTONE BOOKS
Vancouver/Berkeley/London

First published in English by Greystone Books in 2023
Originally published in Norway in 2017 by Cappelen Damm
as *Gutten og fjellet - En oppdagelsesreise i norsk natur*
English translation copyright © 2023 by Becky L. Crook
Photos copyright © 2023 by Torbjørn Ekelund

23 24 25 26 27   5 4 3 2 1

Greystone Books Ltd.
greystonebooks.com

Cataloguing data available from Library and Archives Canada
ISBN 978-1-77164-509-6 (cloth)
ISBN 978-1-77164-510-2 (epub)

Copy editing by Lucy Kenward
Proofreading by Kankana Basu
Jacket design by Belle Wuthrich
Text design by Fiona Siu
Jacket photograph by Torbjørn Ekelund
Printed and bound in Canada
on FSC® certified paper by Friesens

Greystone Books thanks the Canada Council for the Arts,
the British Columbia Arts Council, the Province of British Columbia
through the Book Publishing Tax Credit, and the Government
of Canada for supporting our publishing activities.

This translation has been published with the financial support of NORLA.

Greystone Books gratefully acknowledges the xʷməθkʷəy̓əm (Musqueam),
Sḵwx̱wú7mesh (Squamish), and sel̓íl̓wətaʔɬ (Tsleil-Waututh) peoples on
whose land our Vancouver head office is located.

See the child.

—Cormac McCarthy, *Blood Meridian*

Child vanished. The 6-year-old son of grocer Torske from Kongsberg has gone missing. He was last seen with his mother in a meadow near the mountains of Skrim. A party of one hundred people has gone to search for the boy—they have found no trace.

—*Nedenæs Amtstidende* (newspaper), July 14, 1894

◇◇◇

M Y SON IS NAMED AUGUST. This book is about him, and about a hike we took together the summer he turned seven. We called it The Expedition. Our hike led us through a deserted mountain range, just the two of us. Whatever we needed we carried on our backs. The tent, sleeping bags, sleeping pads and gear, the backpacks heavy with all our supplies. The terrain was hilly and the weather was bad. We scarcely saw another soul.

The region where we undertook our expedition is called Skrim. Just south of the town of Kongsberg, it is considered Norway's smallest connected mountain range. It covers thirteen square miles, large portions of which are protected. The landscape is craggy. The trail is up and down the whole way, which makes for difficult hiking. Even the Skrim massif, the largest of the Skrim mountains, comprises multiple high peaks. The highest of these is called Styggemann, which literally translates as "The Ugly Man." Styggemann is 2,860 feet above sea level, which isn't very high, all things considered. But compared to the surrounding landscape, it is a colossus.

The aim of our expedition was to reach the top of Styggemann. For an adult, this would mean an average day hike from our starting point if one followed the shortest route.

But we were not going to follow the shortest route. We were going to follow whichever route we felt like, taking whatever time we might need, pitching the tent in the evening and then continuing on the next day.

For August, this expedition was an adventure. It was wilderness in its purest form: sleeping in a tent, building a campfire, climbing a mountain, and whittling sticks. It was an adventure for me too, but I also had another motive. There was something I wished to uncover, something that had occupied my thoughts for quite some time and that I was unable to shake.

It was a story I'd come across by chance. A story about a boy who had lost his way in these same mountains over one hundred years ago. The boy's name was Hans Torske. He was six when he disappeared, almost the same age as August.

The details I had managed to glean from the few written sources I'd found were sparse. I thought about Hans Torske day and night, this tiny person in the great wild. I could not get him out of my head.

◇◇◇

I T IS MIDSUMMER. The year is 1894. In the midst of a vast, desolate landscape, a boy is walking. Against the backdrop of trees and mountains, his silhouette is no more than a pinprick, a miniature human figure. The air is warm. He is wearing shorts, a shirt, and a jacket. On his head is a hat. On his feet: no shoes.

He walks alone. Through underbrush and over bogs, along ridges and across streams. The woods are dark, the field is damp. It is blanketed with moss and ferns. The moss dampens his footsteps. The undergrowth brushes his shoulders. He walks along the gleaming bedrock that is rough and warm, almost white in the sunlight.

He turns to look out over the landscape. Far below he can see meadows and patches of land, and his hometown of Kongsberg. That is where he lives with his mother, father, and older brother. He used to have three other siblings but all of them have died.

His father and brother stayed behind in the city; only he and his mother traveled out to stay near the alpine meadow. His mother has tuberculosis. She needed rest and fresh air; that's why they have come. And today is his birthday. Or was it yesterday? He cannot remember how many days have passed since he left the meadow and got lost in the mountains. He is turning six. They were going to have the party out in the meadow, and his big brother had made a wooden sailboat for him as a gift. But the little brother doesn't know this as he stands gazing north toward the farms, the city, which is his salvation.

He looks around. He doesn't know where he is. It has been a long time since he last knew where he was. He can't remember where he turned, which direction he chose, or if he ever turned at all. Maybe he has been walking in a straight line the whole time? Maybe he has been walking in circles? This landscape is unfamiliar; he has never been here before.

He continues up, always up. One mountain peak after another. Trees, swamps—it all looks the same. The hours pass. He feels tired. He drinks his fill in a stream. He finds a handful of berries that help with the worst of the hunger.

It grows darker. The boy continues walking upward. On and on. Walk. Turn. Stop again. Perhaps he cries. Perhaps he calls out. Perhaps he realizes he will never find his way home.

◇◇◇

I HAVE TWO CHILDREN: a daughter who is ten and a son who is seven. They were babies once, helpless little creatures who hardly seemed human. They could neither walk nor speak. They were incapable of caring for themselves and were wholly dependent on someone else. Both are bigger now. They've developed a command of many skills and are gaining more all the time. Nonetheless, I can't help feeling that they are still helpless. I am overwhelmed by the fear of all that could befall them, the many dangers that exist in the world. I do everything in my power to protect them, at all times, every single day. I am aware that they require freedom to learn. That we must give them space to have their own experiences so they can one day be confident. They will not always be children. They will grow up, they will become adults like us.

I know all of this.

And yet I continue to watch over them with vigilance.

I cannot let go.

I was once a child too. It was someone else's job to care for and raise me. At times I look back on my life and wonder what made me the person I am today. Was it my parents' values, my surroundings, friends, school, or the era in which I grew up?

I can remember all of these things. But one thing in particular stands out, and in retrospect it appears more meaningful than all the others: the experience of learning to be in the wild, and the intrinsic value of nature. This sense of the wild took root early on in my life. I came to understand that nature is important for humans, and that it plays a part in regulating our lives for better or worse. The interrelatedness between humans and nature was at the core of my family's worldview. Nature, we believed, was essential for all life on earth, including our own. We knew we depended on it, not only as a source of food but also for perspective, experiences, freedom, and joy. Nature could be mild at times but it could also be ruthless. Above all, nature demanded our respect.

In the beginning, my relationship to nature was intuitive and wordless. It has since grown into something more articulate, something having to do with identity. It is the closest I am able to come to defining who I am. As a child, I loved being outdoors. I felt at home there. I felt that I was good at that kind of life, that I understood it, and in a strange way that I belonged to it. But the years passed, and as I grew older I forgot all of this, or it was relegated to the background. My innate sense of the natural world was forced to give way to other matters that seemed more important in those days, perhaps rightly so.

Shortly after my own children were born, however, I was reminded of the most valuable function of nature in our human lives. This realization didn't come immediately, because in the beginning I had a lot of other things to think about. Everything about having children was new to me. I had a lot to learn about changing diapers and establishing sleep routines and other topics I'd never even considered before. But early on, I was struck by just how much these tiny creatures seemed to enjoy being outside. It was remarkable to me that long before they could walk, they delighted in crawling around on the ground, wrapping their small chubby fists around something, lifting it up, examining it, shoving it into their mouths, and spitting it out or else swallowing it. Sticks and flies and earthworms and rocks—there was nothing that wasn't interesting. And for those of us who stood observing them, it was apparent that this way of being was deeply rooted in the nature of these small humans. It wasn't a skill to be learned or taught. All that was required was for us to open the door and let them outside. The rest worked itself out.

We spent a lot of time outside. Often right in front of our house, in the garden, in the nearby forest, or at our cabin by the lake. The kids didn't require much, only access to the natural world, a place that had not been cultivated for human use or adapted for play, a place they could discover and explore entirely on their own.

And they did. They explored their surroundings and discovered the correlations—tactile, visual, auditory, every kind—between great and small causes and effects. Insignificant flecks of wild nature that an adult might not even notice could occupy the children for hours. And while I observed them, I remembered doing the same thing as a child.

There was nothing I loved more than immersing myself in a minute task for what felt like hours. Following a line of ants along a pine branch to see where it led. Standing on the wharf and staring down at tiny perch sinking and rising slowly in the water, their pectoral fins quivering. When this happened, I forgot about everything else. The only moment that existed was the one unfolding right before my eyes.

It was *being* in its purest form.

For this reason, I take an active role in teaching my children to notice nature's diversity, its processes, its developments; to see the relationships between nature's many components; and to gain an understanding of how these linked lives depend on and influence each other and how nature as a whole—the great machinery—disposes of all living beings in a way that is self-sustaining and renewable.

Such a deep existential understanding of nature is not something that can be absorbed in a classroom or gleaned from the internet. It comes from experiences made up of brief flashes of emotions, experiences you carry your entire life, whose significance expands as you age and plays a part in shaping who you become.

Such realizations would never have been possible if you hadn't been introduced to the natural world when you were a child; for example, by crawling along a wet forest path and shoveling snails and worms into your mouth, or hiking with your dad that summer you turned seven.

Skrim is the name of the barren mountain between Kongsberg and Skien. Although not very tall—it's less than 3,000 feet above sea level—it is nevertheless known for its wildness. Sharp, precipitous peaks rise over the endless marshlands. (...) Standing atop one of these, you can see out over the others, and you might be lured into believing that it's easy to pass between them. If you start to walk, however, you almost always find yourself stuck. The terrain between the peaks is full of deep crevices and ravines, and around them lies an infinity of dark mountain lakes and sinister marshes that give the landscape a trollish, threatening ambience. More than one soul has lost their way in this terrain over the years (...) Even those from the nearby town, hunters and fishers who know the region as they know their own living rooms, can never be certain of not going astray. If bad weather and fog happen to close in, a hiker is lucky if they aren't forced to stay outside and seek shelter beneath a branch or a crag for one night, or more.

—Andreas Eriksen, "Hansemann i Skrim," *Telemark Arbeiderblad* (newspaper), August 20, 1950

AUGUST WAS FOUR the first time he slept in a tent. It was a rainy summer night in the Nordmarka forest, north of Oslo. It was just the two of us.

It was not a long hike. Even so, I had to carry him on my shoulders for much of the way to the campsite, and for even more of the way back. Sometimes, though, he decided he wanted to walk, and when he did, I followed him through the green forest, studying his behavior. He never walked in a straight line but was constantly veering back and forth. He picked up every loose object he came across, which was not an insignificant number. He tried pushing over large trees or pulling them up by the roots. He climbed on boulders that jutted up out of the ground. He tripped and fell and got back up again. He was unable to evaluate distance or to regulate his energy.

If he was in a good mood and felt strong, he ran.

If he felt he couldn't go on, he stopped and lay down on the ground.

He complained endlessly about being tired or wet or cold, and when we got back home the next day I worried for a while that the experience had traumatized him. But it hadn't. In the months that followed, he often spoke about our camping trip in the woods and without a trace of bitterness. It seemed he had forgotten all of the inconveniences and only remembered the good parts.

"I want to go again," he told me.

And so we did.

The following summer we ventured out on several overnight trips, all of them short and manageable. August turned five; he turned six.

One dark autumn evening, I said to him: "Should we plan to go on a real expedition, just the two of us?"

He replied: "Yes! When? Now?"

I said, "No, not now. We have to wait until next summer. When you finish first grade, then I think you'll be big enough."

I explained it was good that next summer was so far away because we had a lot of planning to do. For instance, we had to figure out where to go. We had to assess our gear, what we already owned and what we still needed to get.

He agreed.

I asked him to write down what outdoor equipment he already had. On a white sheet of paper, he wrote the word KNIFE with the K facing the wrong way. This was his entire list. The summer he turned five I'd bought him a scout knife with light red leather trim and a lacquered pale wooden handle with red paint at one end. It wasn't much, but if we had been living 300 years ago, I might have thought this was sufficient.

August seemed disappointed.

"All you need is a loin cloth and then you'll have as much as Tarzan," I told him.

"That's not funny," he said.

He sat on the couch with his nearly blank page before him. I could see his wheels spinning, and soon he was able to remember other items that he had. He wrote them down too, with a bit of assistance from me:

SLEEPING BAG

FISHING ROD

CAMP SHOES

WATER BOTTLE

In the weeks that followed, we hatched our plan. I enjoy planning and envisioning future events. August, however, has very little to do with the past or future. He might push himself so far as to ask how long it is until the weekend, or what we did yesterday. But beyond that, he spends the majority of his time in the present. Planning is thus an unbearable activity for him.

Autumn turned into winter. August forgot about The Expedition and lost himself in other things. But I didn't forget. In the evenings, after he was in bed, I sat with maps unfolded across the kitchen table, studying them in the yellow light of the lamp.

I was considering several different locations.

The Hardanger Plateau.

Femundsmarka National Park.

Børgefjell National Park.

Rondane National Park.

Then my eyes fell across Skrim. A small mountain region for a small boy. It was here, in this landscape, that our expedition would take place.

I BEGAN TO PREPARE. I took stock of our gear. Noted down what we still needed, ordered books about Skrim, about the fauna and flora and geology and history. I had a map. It was from the 1970s, creased and worn, inherited from my father and apparently the same map we had used when I was a child. I checked if there were any updated versions of the map and found that there were. *Hiking and Ski Maps for Skrim* was a revised edition of the map from the 1970s. This one was printed in color, and on the back were historical tidbits and practical information.

My attention was drawn to a note with the heading "Monuments." A short way down the text, I read:

> *Hans Torske was six when he got lost on his way from Breistul pasture to Styggemann peak. A search party was sent out. Without success. (...) Similar more recent situations have led to the conclusion that children have an incredible amount of stamina and are able to cover a large radius if motivated. Children who have lost their way also tend to head uphill— possibly because it makes them feel safer ...*

I studied the map and the region north of Styggemann peak. At the base of the mountain, where the landscape flattened out, were three alpine pastures, each with scattered buildings. One of the pastures was called Breistulseter. As the bird flies, there was less than a mile or so between Breistul pasture and Styggemann, but the contour lines on the map indicated that the terrain was steep and the elevation gain between the pasture and the top of the mountain might even be over 1,500 feet.

Something in me clicked. The historical note on the map sounded so authoritative, almost genial, as if the disappearance of a child was a frequent occurrence in the Skrim mountains.

I couldn't push the thought of this boy from my mind. It wasn't so much the fact that he must have been hungry and cold, but that he had been all alone. I pictured him in the vast landscape, tiny and exhausted. Wanting to go home, but not knowing which way to go. He wanted someone to help him, but no one could help him because no one knew where he was.

The boy was the embodiment of a universal condition of existence: nature's crushing superiority and the smallness of humankind in the face of it. The boy in the footnote stood for all of us.

And just like that The Expedition took on a double aim.

◇◇◇

I T IS ONE OF THE LIGHTEST DAYS of the year. We are
standing in a parking lot at the end of a gravel road. To
the east, the sheer face of a mountain looms skyward.
To our west is a pond with lines rippling in the mild afternoon breeze. Before us are the Skrim mountains.

Before parking, we stopped at the kiosk at the base of the
valley to purchase a fishing license. The kiosk was like all
such kiosks: the stub of a pencil inside a weatherworn box
under a bulletin board adorned with bits of torn pages
and rusty thumbtacks. Inside the wooden box were damp
envelopes in which to put the money for the license, and
beneath it an iron canister with a tiny slit in it. A fishing
license costs next to nothing, but judging by the thickness
of the iron, it must have contained millions. We stuffed
the money into the envelope and shoved the envelope into
the canister. Placed the stubby pencil back in the box and
drove on.

The parking lot is empty. There are no other cars. Presumably because the official start of summer vacation is a few
weeks away, most people are still at work.
    We park, lace up our hiking boots, and heave our back-
packs onto our backs.

August's backpack is blue and clean and almost unused. His grandpa gave it to him for Christmas. It can hold up to 15 liters and stretches from his lower back up to the middle of his blond head. The backpack isn't very big, but then neither is August.

He's a mere 53 pounds.

No more than four feet or so above the ground.

A recent graduate of the first grade.

He no longer writes his Ks the wrong way. He is bigger now, but in light of what lies before us, I am not convinced he's big enough.

My own backpack is as tall as August and weighs more than he does. My pack can hold 100 liters. We've packed as little as possible, but for the shoulders of a single adult, it's more than enough.

I've brought along my hiking poles. The intention is to use them as extra support for my enormous backpack, but now August tells me he wants to use them. I adjust the poles down to his height.

I check to make sure the car is locked. I've never left it for this long in the middle of the forest; just the thought makes me nervous. I push the lock button on my key fob and then check the door handle. I do it one more time.

"You already checked it," says August.

"I know," I say.

I put the key fob in my pocket, but then I change my mind, take my backpack off and set it on the ground. I stick the key into a zippered pocket under the top flap of the pack, but not before checking one last time that the car is indeed locked. Then I pull shut the zipper, secure the flap of the backpack, and lift the straps back onto my shoulders.

August gapes at me.

Then we start walking.

We pass a barrier, a bollard, that prevents cars from driving farther along the gravel road. August pads off with his hiking poles and blue backpack, with a lightness that lets me know he is content with life. I've been here before; I know what lies ahead. August is on his way into the unknown. I follow behind. I think about the hobbit Sam in *The Lord of the Rings*. After he and Frodo have been given their dangerous assignment, when the long journey begins and he is standing on the edge of the field that is the boundary to Hobbiton, Sam says:

If I take one more step, it will be the farthest away from home I've ever been.

THERE ARE MANY POSSIBLE STARTING POINTS for an excursion into the Skrim mountains. Ours begins on the eastern edge, from the valley where the Numesdalslågen river twists and winds toward the city of Larvik and the sea.

After half a mile, we arrive at one of Skrim's many mountain huts. Although no one is there, we can see that it is frequently visited. The main building is large and painted black. Canoes and boats are tied up along the shore. The cabin is at the southern end of a lake. The northern side of the lake is where the mountain range begins, leading to its highest point, Styggemann. We can't see the top now, but we know it is there behind the hills.

It may be three days' journey away.

It may be five.

Or seven.

Or we may turn around and never reach it at all.

It depends on how we look at it. The outcome is dependent on a variety of factors and relationships: weather and motivation, health and our physical shape, but I believe we are prepared well enough to face most things. And we have enough time; time is not a factor.

I have tried to imagine how it must feel to experience this hike as a seven-year-old. When I was August's age, my family lived in a forested area—and inside of this forested area was an open plain. There was a soccer field and a hill that we could ski down in the winter. I have since returned to that place as an adult. The hill is not very big, and it was not very far away from where our house used to be. But I was struck by how big the forest actually is, even though the opposite is usually true. Namely, that when adults revisit things that we recall as being big in our childhood, we are often surprised at how small they are in reality.

The forest of my childhood was the opposite. It was much larger than I'd remembered, and even though we'd passed through it every day after school, I don't think we'd ever crossed its entire expanse. We'd always walked to a particular point and then stopped. We'd harbored an instinctive respect for the forest. Maybe it was a fear of the unknown that cautioned us from venturing farther—the idea that if we kept going we would cross an invisible line and, without realizing it, find ourselves in the territory of strangers, whoever those people were who lived on the opposite side of the forest and whom we did not know.

I myself have been to the top of Styggemann. August has never been there, but he has thought a lot about the top of the mountain and is eager. It is not totally clear what, specifically, he is eager about. Presumably about standing on the very top. Children often dream about that moment when the toil will be over and the victory secured. They like to watch the award ceremonies for sporting events on TV, especially the moment when the athletes hoist their trophies into the air. August invariably dreams of extremely successful outcomes. He is always the hero in his own stories.

We take a break at the mountain hut. We lean our backpacks against two trees and sit down on a log that has been sawed in half and placed by a campfire pit to use as a bench. We drink from our water bottles and eat peanuts.

August has discovered a chaffinch hopping about on the wet soil while looking aslant at us. August wants to give it peanuts. I say that might not be such a good idea because the nuts are salty, and salt isn't good for birds. I suspect he nonetheless slips a few peanuts to the bird before we continue on our way. It will survive. If it gets thirsty, there's an entire lake available.

We continue our trek along a clearly marked path. We turn to look at the mountain hut. This is the moment when we leave the final bit of civilization, and for the first time the terrain through which we will pass in the coming days becomes visible. Marshes and bogs bedecked with bilberry shrubs and cloudberry blossoms. Large, flat mountain ranges. Dwarf birch, pine, and gnarled old fir trees.

The word *skrim* comes from Old Norse and means "dim light." The verb *skrima* means "to show oneself obscurely" or "to appear as dark." There are other theories as to the meaning of these words and why the Skrim mountains were given this name, but the first one fits with the reality of it. Viewed from the city of Kongsberg to the north and the surrounding farmland, the Skrim mountain range looms like a dark shadow above the landscape. It hovers behind the forest in the southwest, a dim mountain formation with Styggemann at its center, sharply drawn against the sky.

"I am starting to feel like I miss home, but I'm not going to give up," August informs me and then keeps walking.

After a few steps more, he stops and turns around to face me. He says: "Now I don't miss home anymore."

We continue on for a long period, he in front and me behind. He swings constantly from one state to another, and I consider how exhausting it must be to be a child. Everything goes faster than it does for adults. Life fluctuates at a tremendous speed. A child can shift from intense happiness to deep despair in such a short period of time, yet during that same period an adult may not have experienced a single emotion, positive or negative. That's just what it's like to be a child. Such a state has its advantages and disadvantages. One disadvantage is that children are not very good at shutting out their worries and stresses. One advantage is that they are able to push them aside the moment these feelings no longer feel urgent.

And then they just keep going.

Onward, toward new victories and defeats.

I think about Hans Torske, the same thought I've had so many times while planning our expedition. He was only six years old. Did he realize he was lost? Was he able to grasp the gravity of his situation? Did he try to search systematically for a way back to his starting point, or did he keep going in the hope that if he walked far enough he'd find his way home?

I have never told August this story. I've thought about telling him, but not now, not at the start of The Expedition. I'm worried it might frighten him. I'll wait for the right moment.

This first leg of our hike takes us through flat, straightforward terrain. We reach a ravine where the path plunges steeply into the woods. Then it comes up again.

When August is in good form, he explores whatever he passes. Adds rocks to the top of cairns, hops over streams, balances on ancient logs. He babbles to himself constantly. An even stream of ideas and thoughts bubbling to the surface. And then he is quiet. We walk for a ways without speaking. I have my own thoughts, but what is August thinking about?

Does he know how far we've walked? Does he know how long it will be before we stop to pitch the tent?

It's not clear. One's sense of time is altered when passing through natural settings where the only marks of humankind are old paths and signposts that have been around for so long they've taken on the colors and textures of the surrounding landscape. Gray, dry, weathered. The signposts look like they've been dragged up from the cellar of time, left over like the gravel and sand and big angular rocks from the last ice age.

Through this landscape walks a boy who recently finished the first grade, who has grown up surrounded by shops and playgrounds and friends at the edge of a large city, who has adapted to an existence in which every day is planned to the last detail and optimized for whatever self-realization someone else has decided is most promising for him. The boy walks now through a wilderness that is indifferent to his presence there. That hasn't been optimized for any purpose whatsoever. That does not care about him and that would not hesitate to take his life if he doesn't watch out and make good decisions.

As August walks ahead of me, I consider that what he is experiencing now is something he can't put to words but will be valuable for the rest of his life. For the first time, he is experiencing being part of a context that is larger than he previously believed. Though he may not realize it yet, he is learning that his role in this context is very brief and that he must use this time to become familiar with nature, to treat it with respect, and to protect it because it provides the conditions for his own and all other living creatures' lives.

◇◇◇◇◇

AUGUST STOPS WALKING and turns to face me again. He pushes his hat back, and his hiking pole swings like a pendulum in front of his face.

"When I'm big, I want to be the same as you," he says.

"That's very nice," I say.

"Yes, it is nice," says August. "But what are you, actually?"

I don't quite know what to reply to that, and so we continue walking in silence across the pine barrens.

The landscape changes constantly. The soil at higher elevations is thin. Pine and birch, blueberry shrubs low to the ground. Open flecks of gray granite covered with map lichen, the greenish-yellow variety of lichen that is very typical in alpine settings and that got its name because it looks like a map spread across the bedrock.

The forest opens up. We make our way across wide, wet bogs. Damp and teeming with life, bogs are an important part of Norwegian nature not only because they provide a habitat for birds, animals, and insects, but also because they store large amounts of carbon. Bogs and marshlands are threatened; they are being drained and turned into arable land, and then replaced by artificial turf and shopping centers and housing developments. When this happens, the stored carbon is released and valuable storage areas are lost.

We are so concerned about protecting the rain forests that they have become symbols of modern environmental activism. Yet there is a certain irony that the natural peat bogs found everywhere in my country, and in other countries, and that are now becoming fewer and fewer, have the same carbon-storage function as rain forests but most of us aren't even aware of it.

August walks quickly and with ease. With my heavy pack, I can hardly keep up. As we descend the terrain, the spruce trees begin to appear. They don't look like the ones in a well-planned nursery. These are scrawnier and there's more space between their branches, which slope toward the ground and are shaggy and stunted. These spruces are reminiscent of pines, large and ancient, like petrified trolls stooping silently along the narrow path.

Carpeting the ground beneath the trees are bone-dry branches that have fallen in storms or under the weight of snow. August gathers these one after the other, apparently to see if he can find a use for them. Since I've had kids, first a girl and then a boy, I've observed them and their friends—in kindergarten, on the sidewalk, on the way to school, or in the woods—and in all of these contexts I have never seen the girls show much interest in sticks. The boys, however, have picked up every stick in sight. Over the course of his young life, August has found and collected hundreds of sticks, whether because they've reminded him of something else or because he thinks they'll come in handy.

Small dry twigs.

Heavy wet sticks.

Brittle light yellow reeds.

Thin new deciduous saplings.

All of these he has collected and stockpiled at home. Every so often we throw them out in utmost secrecy. If we did not do this, our home would be crammed full of sticks.

LATE IN THE AFTERNOON, after several hours of walking and a few erroneous detours, we arrive at the lake where we are going to set up camp. We have passed several other lakes and ponds along the way, but they were in the middle of floating peat bogs and therefore impossible to put a tent on. As the crow flies, the lake is only a few miles southwest of the parking lot where we left the car but the paths in this area don't go as the crow flies. I estimate that we have walked for a good five or six miles, at least.

We scout out a good spot for the tent on a spit in one of the lake's many small inlets. The ground here is flat enough to pitch the tent so it is level. As an added bonus, a little outcrop of rock extends into the water like a piece of coastal bedrock. It will make a nice spot for sitting, come evening.

Behind us in the forest we hear birdsong, and from the heather comes the hum of a thousand insects. A mild breeze from the south ripples over the water. The waves clap against the rocky outcropping. It hasn't rained all day but the air has been heavy and humid.

We get out the tent.

I spent a lot of time trying to find just the right model, and I ended up with a three-person dome tent. It's free-standing, which is a good thing if the ground is too hard to drive in the stakes. The fact that it can house three adults means there's space for our gear if it starts to rain.

We assemble the tent. August has helped me set it up before, and so he knows what has to be done.

Unfold the tent body on the ground.

Put together the three poles: one blue, one gray, and one orange.

Insert the poles into the right pole sleeves and grommets in the tent body, made easy because of the cor-responding colors.

Set the tent on the ground and drive in the stakes.

And, finally, attach the rainfly.

We blow up our sleeping pads and unroll the sleeping bags to air them out. Fill the tent with things we will need when it's bedtime. Donald Duck comics, books, headlamps, and water bottles. The wind shifts from south to north and grows stronger. Dark clouds pile up overhead. The lake's surface is cold and metallic.

We call home. Not because we are homesick but because we promised to turn on the cell phone every eve-ning after setting up camp so those at home will know that we are okay. I want to test whether or not August knows how to make a call. If anything were to happen, it's a com-fort to know that he would be able to contact someone.

His tiny fingers fly across the smartphone keys faster than I am able to follow. They punch in the password, look up contacts, find Trude, push the call button and then the speakerphone.

Seconds later, Mom is on the line. She tells August she's at a party and that his big sister, Helena, is spending the night at a friend's. She asks how we're doing. August tells her everything we've done. I can hear the pride in his voice, but there's also a measure of despondency over the fact that he can't quite express just how different this life is from the one at home. For his mother, it's just another day. For August, it's a day in a tent in a place he's never been before in his whole life.

IN THE EVENING, we cook tomato soup and macaroni on the Primus stove. The air is thick with midges and mosquitoes. The mosquitoes are nothing compared to the midges, which find their way into every orifice. They are an invisible, invincible enemy. August scratches his head frantically; his face is covered in bites, tiny red dots, and he looks like he's got the measles.

We build a smoker to keep the midges at bay. I've brought along a tin can. I poke holes around the can toward the bottom to create a draft. August looks for birchbark, sticks, and dry pine needles. He puts the bark and twigs in the bottom of the can. Then he lights them. Once the flames have caught, he fills the can with pinecones. Thick white smoke billows upward. It envelops his whole head in a cloud, but at least it keeps the midges away.

We spend the next few hours fishing for trout. We get five bites but aren't able to reel any of them in. August does not have the same patience for fishing that I did at his age. He thinks it's fun, but he soon grows bored if nothing bites. I continue to fish. August plays with two ants. He has placed them on a large rock surrounded by water on all sides. He gives them names. One is Billy and the other is Larsen.

He says out loud to himself: "Larsen drowns in a storm and now Billy is all alone." He adds: "It's okay during the day, but when it's nighttime he thinks about Larsen. In the end, Billy commits suicide."

When it is dark, we go into the tent. We've brought along Grandpa's old edition of Daniel Defoe's famous novel *Robinson Crusoe*. On the title page, in black cursive writing, is the name Pål Lorentzen. One can read into the script that this signature belongs to a boy who seldom has the chance to write his name in books and has thus taken great care in doing it.

I start reading.

"What does it mean to fall in battle?" August asks without being particularly interested.

I start to reply but he interrupts me and says he would rather read his Donald Duck comics. I get it. The funniest of the stories is about two hillbilly families who have been enemies for generations, men with long beards and flannel shirts fighting about which family owns the forest where they live.

We read until August says he would like to go to bed. Five minutes later, he's asleep. He is type A like me, enthusiastic from his waking moment but as soon as it's evening time, he grows tired and loses faith in just about everything. When his head hits the pillow, he drops off almost instantaneously.

It starts to rain. Lightly at first, and then more heavily. I zip open the tent and peek out. The landscape is different than it was when we came into the tent. The fog and mist form so I can just make out the water; the spruce trees behind the tent are barely visible. I close the zipper and listen to the rain drumming against the fly.

Once the children are asleep, the adults tidy up. This is as true on a camping trip as it is at home. Tent life requires you stay organized so you'll know where to find things when you need them.

Rain clothes.

Headlamp.

Knife.

First-aid kit.

A boy of seven is not primarily concerned about keeping things in order. He wishes to do everything at once. Whittle sticks. Blow up his sleeping pad. Put his knife down on his sleeping pad. Start on some other activity.

I organize our backpacks and put everything into its right place. I think we've brought too many things. Too many clothes. Too much food. The backpacks are too heavy. My lower back aches.

I look over at August asleep in his sleeping bag.

I am always worried but I don't think he feels the same way. This is his usual state. He doesn't live according to the clock or the weather report, but rather he relies on others—preferably his parents—to make decisions on his behalf. He has spent his entire life blindly trusting us as messengers of good and bad news about our surroundings, prospects, and life in general.

That's what it is to be seven years old. It is a life in which others call the shots. One is not necessarily free, but at least one is safe. August snores in his sleeping bag. He has complete trust that I will lead him through these days of wandering and deliver him safely back home, to his mom and sister, Helena, and the cat and his life as he knows it.

◇◇◇

Picture a boy in a tent in a forest. The forest is old; it has always been there. The boy is seven; he is here for the first time.

It is evening. The trees are ringed with vapor. The rain beats down on the rainfly of the tent. The boy is sleeping. He turns in his sleep. Scratches his cheek, swats away insects in his dream, pulls the sleeping bag over his head. His body is covered with bites from mosquitoes and blackflies. His arms, legs, temples, chest.

His father is taking notes in the white light of his headlamp. He gazes down at the sleeping boy and thinks: we are the only two humans in these woods and no one knows where we are. He sits for a long time before putting away his notebook. Finally, he turns off the headlamp and creeps down into his sleeping bag.

Soon they are both asleep, and outside the rain falls in the big, dark forest.

◇◇◇

P ICTURE A MORNING in a tent in a forest. A blond head
inside a sleeping bag. Squinted eyes. Suntanned skin.
A puzzled expression before he realizes where he is.
The boy looks up and smiles. Remembers. In a tent in a forest, that's where we are. He inches over toward his father
and lays his head on his father's chest.

"I had a dream," says the boy, "about the ants on the rock
and someone in my class."

"Did you?" says the father. "I didn't dream at all, but
before I fell asleep I thought how we are the only people
in the woods and no one knows where we are. Now I'm
wondering what kind of weather it is outside and where
we are going to hike today."

The boy smiles. He is listening for rain but he can't hear
any.

They lie there for a long time like that.

Two people in an old forest.

In a tent beyond time.

The grocer Torske's six-year-old son was with his mother at a summer pasture on Skrim where they were staying for health reasons. He disappeared on Sunday afternoon when he was left alone for a few moments on the stairs at the foot of the farmhouse door. When the little boy was not found, a search party from town was immediately organized to help search the area. The first night, approximately 100 people from surrounding farms came to help. Later reinforcements from the city included many of Torske's former colleagues from the weapons factory where he'd once worked, so there were often around fifty people searching at any given time. However, no trace has yet been found of the boy.

The disappearance has spurred most of the city's inhabitants into action to help the grieving parents, for whom the loss would be very hard.

The current mild weather means the missing child might yet be found alive and without permanent injury.

—*Kongsberg Adresse* (newspaper), July 12, 1894

◇◇◇

BREISTULSETER IS THE NAME of a high mountain pasture north of Skrim. It is situated at the base of the steep slopes leading up to the mountain. Although the wide-open meadow may have looked different in Hans Torske's day, it is nevertheless still there. Sections of the area have been modernized, but some of the original buildings are still standing. These structures are small and simple granaries or hay barns built of thick, notched logs, with small windows and low doors.

It was to this mountain pasture area that Hans Torske went that summer with his mother, apparently around Midsummer Eve. The family usually resided in the city of Kongsberg, a dozen miles away, so mother and son must have arrived by horse and cart. It was not unusual for city dwellers to spend time in the mountain pastures throughout the summer as a retreat from urban life.

His father, Haagen Torske, and older brother, Erik, stayed behind in Kongsberg. Hans's father was born in 1847 and his mother in 1854, which meant they were forty-seven and forty years old respectively that summer. According to church records, the couple had five children together, three of whom had died young. The two living children were Erik and Hans. It was the younger brother, Hans, who'd accompanied his mother to the pasture. It's possible they had been there before, though perhaps not. In any case, as a city boy, Hans was more than likely unfamiliar with spending time outdoors.

Several versions suggest what might have transpired on the day Hans vanished. One version says he was sent off to meet a shepherdess who was leading her flock toward the evening pen. Another tells that he and his mother had quarreled, that Hans was upset, and that he stomped off without a trace. A third version has it that he was left alone outside on the farmhouse steps for mere moments. A fourth says that the boy was last seen playing in the farmyard and that when he was called in for dinner a short while later, there was no reply. His mother went outside to look for him, but the yard was empty and the boy had vanished. It was afternoon or early evening.

A stable high-pressure system hovered over the eastern part of Norway on that day. The weather was calm and the temperature warm. In such mild conditions, a six-year-old boy visiting a mountain pasture with his mother at the end of the 1800s would have been clad in simple summer clothing.

A shirt and short pants.

A thin jacket.

A cap on his head.

And he is barefoot.

It's easy to imagine him as Emil of Lönneberga from Astrid Lindgren's series of children's books, climbing a rail fence or running through knee-high grass across the meadows.

There's no longer any living witness who can say exactly how the events unfolded out on Breistul pasture that summer evening, or how many people were in fact present. At some point, someone must have realized that the boy really was missing. That he wasn't just going to reappear among the meadow flowers where he had been innocently lying on his back studying the clouds. That he wasn't going to pop up from behind the timber barn with a kitten in his arms.

Why did he leave?

Was he chasing a butterfly? Had he squeezed his eyes shut to experience what it's like to walk around blind? Did he hear a bird singing in the woods and follow the sound to find out what kind of bird it was? Or had he merely ambled away, lost in his own thoughts, the way six-year-olds so often do, blissfully unaware that it's much easier to enter the forest than to find your way out again?

It's not hard to imagine the mother's reaction when she realized her son was missing. A primal reaction not bound to time or culture or class or religion, a spontaneous reflex set in motion by that most powerful of instincts: the urge to protect one's offspring. A stab in the chest, a spreading panic, a fear of every calamity that might befall a child, but also a voice that says, "Calm down, take it easy, it's happened many times before, he's probably very close by, he's only a child, he is going to show up."

The minutes that tick past, the panic that increases. The voice that continues to soothe but starts to sound less and less confident.

Where should we start the search?

This is the question that the boy's mother and anyone else on Breistul pasture that day must have begun asking when they realized he really was missing. People gathered quickly from the surrounding area to join the search. They must have organized themselves rapidly because there is not much distance between the farms. Ten minutes at a walk. Three minutes at a run.

To start, they might not have had a concrete plan. They might simply have run in all directions, calling out, their voices increasingly louder, fanning out farther and farther from the farm, their desperation growing. Later on, several hundred people came from Kongsberg, mostly workers from the weapons factory and the silver mine.

Someone must have taken the lead and outlined a plan for how they would continue the search. The mother must have been consulted about her small child's personality and behavior, whether or not something unusual had happened in the days prior that could shed light on where he could have gone. The search party must have studied each major direction, trying to decide which explanation was most probable about where the boy might have headed. And they must have probed his mother about the boy's experience in the outdoors, in the forest, and on mountains; about whether he had spent a lot of time outside, and about whether he was strong and persistent. But first and foremost, they must have considered the local terrain and what could pose a threat to the boy's life and well-being.

To the north of the pasture lay vast swaths of forest and agricultural lands. This was also the direction in which it was easiest to walk and reach other developments in the shortest distance. To the east, the terrain was very similar at first but soon began to slope down toward the valley and the city of Kongsberg. To the south were the steep mountain foothills leading upward toward the Skrim massif, alpine terrain that was only rarely visited and through which it was inconceivable that a small boy might pass. To the west ran a river, and this was where the search party decided to look first.

More help arrived. They walked fanned out in a straight line. They probed the river. They combed the forest. They scrambled on hands and feet up the steep slopes leading toward Skrim.

Their labor was fruitless. Hans Torske had seemingly vanished into thin air.

In the first days, the newspaper announcements were optimistic. But as the days passed, they were no longer hopeful. Instead, they took on an undertone of quiet resignation.

◇◇◇

To wake in a tent in the woods is not the same as waking up in a bed in a house, where stirring to the sound of an alarm can sometimes feel like rising from the dead. The warm coziness of the bed poses the starkest possible contrast to the wooden floor's cold surface. You do not want to put your feet down on it; you would like to stay curled up beneath the comforter.

In a tent, things are different. You are always aware of your surroundings, even when you're asleep. The scrunch of the sleeping bag fabric when you turn over. The contours of the ground beneath your thin sleeping pad. And the noises outside. The scattered chirping of birds throughout the night. The wind that makes tree branches move and leaves rustle softly. The buzzing of mosquitoes. The patter of raindrops.

There is no alarm clock in the tent. You wake when your body decides it's time. Perhaps roused by a sunbeam that slants through the foliage and illuminates the interior space where you are lying. Or by a sound outside the tent that gradually crescendos louder and louder, signaling the morning.

I open my eyes and find myself looking straight at August's face. He is awake. His Buff bandanna is on his head. He is smiling and I return the smile. It's unclear how long he's been lying like that, or what he is thinking about. Neither of us speaks.

Outside it is quiet. I listen for noises that can tell us what the weather might be, but I hear nothing. This suggests the sun is not up yet, and also that the rain has stopped. I don't know what time it is, nor do I care to find out. It may be five or seven or nine o'clock. It doesn't matter.

We study the map. We decide to continue on a westward course. There is a small mountain plateau in that direction that we would like to see. Our plan doesn't extend any farther than that. Once we reach the mountain plateau, we can hatch a new plan.

Breaking camp when everything is wet is not what I consider one of life's most pleasurable tasks. The best way to go about it is to pack all that you possibly can while still inside the tent. Sleeping bags, sleeping pads, food, and gear. Next, put on the clothes you plan to wear that day, and only after everything else has been packed away do you go outside and take down the tent.

Doing this alone is one thing. Doing it with a child is quite another. Children rarely understand the kind of systematic order that such situations demand. But August is clever. He has been out with me before, and in more demanding conditions than this: heavy rainfall, thick autumnal darkness, sub-zero temperatures.

We go about things in the proper order. August is in a good mood, as he always is in the morning.

I pack up the tent while he prepares breakfast.
Oatmeal on the Primus stove.
Butter, sugar, and cinnamon.
Hot cocoa for him.
Coffee for me.

It has rained more than I realized. The air is cold and biting.
The temperature is just above freezing, a reminder that it
can get very cold even in the middle of summer.

We pull on our long johns and shell pants, shell jackets,
bandannas, hats, and gloves. The fog cloaks the water like a
thick blanket. The rain has made the ground wet and muddy.
Ten thousand pine needles from last season and even before
that stick to the sides of the tent and to our backpacks
and pants and boots, and on the heather that reaches to
August's knees, icy raindrops gleam in the morning light.

We make our way through forests and over mountains.
August carries the map around his neck; he is the one primarily responsible for our navigation.

The wind blows from the north. It picks up speed.

When we reach the mountain plateau, which was the
goal of this stage, we snack on nuts and study the map
again. August takes out his little compass, which we bought
at a sporting goods store for an alarmingly low price.

"Where should we go next?" I ask.

"There is north," August replies, pointing to the south.

New landscape, new paths. Some notable things we
encounter along the way: a stick that looks like a human,

an anthill that is taller than a boy, ripe blueberries, and a bird alighting from the marsh. The rhythm that rises when walking. The sense of all time ceasing.

No one type of landscape prevails on Skrim. Walk five miles in any direction and you will encounter it all. The upper regions are dominated by scraggly, windswept spruce, pine, and dwarf birch trees, loose gravel, and sand. But as we descend, conditions become as fertile as in any rain forest.

Towers of stones—cairns—are everywhere, some of them piled up right next to each other. It's hard to understand why anyone would decide to stack stones directly beside another stack in a desolate mountain landscape, but that's what happens it seems. Where there's one cairn, there are often dozens. Maybe the builders of these stacks felt somewhat lonely as they meandered along, and this loneliness expressed itself in building new neighboring cairns. Perhaps this is how cities have formed.

Whenever August feels tired and discouraged, he knocks the cairns over. When his mood is lighter, he adds to them, stacking the stones higher. Every so often he stops and turns to face me because he has something weighing on him, a serious declaration he needs to make or an important question to ask. His reservoir is infinite. I make the mistake of mentioning the ice age, and now he wants to know more about it. I tell him as much as I know, as much as I can remember, and some things I simply make up on the spot, but this hardly matters to my listener.

The first sign of life on earth was a mindless green blob of biomass hundreds of millions of years ago, I tell him, but to keep things simple, let's just say that everything started with the ice age, the one that ended about ten thousand years ago. That was the beginning of our world as we know it—humans with big heads and big brains living together in a society; who are constantly developing and improving our surroundings, tools and technology, and forms of entertainment; who have an artistic need for expression; and who, though they try really hard to distribute resources evenly among themselves, rarely succeed. They argue and fight, within their own groups and with other groups, because there's always someone who wants more than everyone else.

August appears engrossed in his compass, but I think he is listening. Children of his generation are intimately connected to this topic because most of them have watched the movie *Ice Age*.

The first thing that happened was that the ice melted. It receded on the land or floated out to sea through valleys before it finally dispersed. The land that had been beneath the ice was revealed and it must have been a wasteland of mountains and stone and scree and sand, not unlike on the moon.

Everything was barren and empty; there were no signs of life. But then the first plants appeared, the seeds presumably carried in bird droppings. The plants must have come before animals, because plants are the cause and animals are the effect. Animals came because the plants were here.

Plant eaters—for example, reindeer—moved north to eat the plants. Meat eaters—for example, bears or wolves—came north to eat the plant eaters.

"And the fish?" asks August.

It's hard to say, I tell him. Maybe they were there beneath the ice the whole time, because the ocean's history is a completely different story.

And then came the humans.

Researchers believe hunters have been in Norway since before the last ice age, twenty thousand years ago, but they have never found any evidence from this period. So, we'll just stick to the past ten thousand years. This period got its name because the tools that humans used were made of stone, bone, flint, and wood. Humans followed the edge of the ice north and migrated to Norway from three very different places. Some came up toward Oslo through the southern tip of the country. Some came to the western part of Norway across the so-called North Sea continent. There was no sea in those days, and so they could walk on dry land where today we have to go by boat. Others immigrated from the east. They arrived, realized that no one else was living there, that the land was open and available, and so they settled down.

At first, humans primarily lived along the coasts, but they soon spread inland and up into the mountains. Some migrated to Skrim, where ancient animal pits have been discovered: pits dug by humans for catching animals. Agriculture had not yet taken root. These humans were still hunters and fishers. For this reason, they didn't stay in one place; they wandered around, following the prey. Large areas of land were needed to find food. In fact, an area as large as the Skrim mountains may have supported only a single human.

The oldest known human skeleton found in Norway was discovered in the town of Søgne, along the southern coast. It was a woman. Her skull was found on the shore by someone vacationing at their cabin not very long ago, and dating shows that she died around 8000 BC. They also uncovered her hip and leg bones. From these fragments, scientists were able to determine that the woman was just over five feet tall and around forty years old when she died. There is a deep gash in her skull, suggesting that she was murdered. Her diet consisted of food from the sea: shellfish, fish, crabs, seals, whales. She lived in a hunter-gatherer culture and her days must have gone something like this:

Wake up hungry.

Catch something.

Eat it.

Rest.

Get hungry again.

Catch something.

Eat it.

Rest.

WE HEAD WEST, in the opposite direction to where the ice flowed in the last ice age.

Our path leads us up and down, up and down.

The wind is calmer in the valley. But it's also wetter there. All of the water that fell overnight has gone where water always goes: to the lowest point. Around us are aspen and rowan trees, moss and ferns. The lush black soil clings to our boots.

We continue on until we reach a small lake. The cloud layer breaks and for the first time all day we are offered a patch of blue sky.

"My feet are soaking," August says. "We'll stop here today."

I take a look at the map to figure out precisely where we are. It's hard to say. We are probably next to one of the little lakes that doesn't have a name because it's too small, or because no one has come up with a good name for it.

I look up from the map.

"This lake doesn't have a name," I say. "Let's call it 'The Nameless Lake.'"

August stares at me with a look that tells me that his imagination has just been activated. I can see it's a name he likes, and I know from experience that this sort of name always appeals to children his age. A single utterance of just such a word, preferably a word with a touch of the sinister, and their young brains run amok.

Nameless.

Strange.

Unknown.

Hidden.

Secret.

They can't get enough of it.

Judging by the position of the sun, it is early afternoon. I had envisioned walking a bit longer, yet the lake does have a pleasant spot for camping and August has already started making himself at home. He's removed his clothes. He sits in his underwear on a slab of bedrock jutting into the water. I can hear him singing a song I've never heard him sing before. Soft tones flitting across the water and mingling with the wind as it rustles the birch leaves.

"Where on earth did you learn that song?" I ask.

"At school," August says.

"Sing it again," I say.

"No," says August.

"Please," I say.

"Okay," says August.

And then he sings, in a voice that is high and clear:

Sea and sky, cheek to cheek.
Seagull nests and seagull shriek.
Motor puff and southern breeze.
Sea spray over slippery reefs.
Small white houses dot the coves.
No more homework. No more clothes.

AUGUST IS BUSY at the water's edge. He babbles happily in the sunshine. When he is playing, he talks to himself, wholly engrossed in his activity. His is a parallel universe, and I let him be. This seems like a good place to let be.

With one eye on August, I take care of those tasks that are best done whenever there is both sunshine and a breeze. Pitch the tent, put all the gear inside, unroll the sleeping bags and air them out over a low pine branch, put up a clothesline, hang all the wet clothes, put out the shoes to dry on the rocks.

It takes a split second to get thoroughly drenched but an eternity to dry off again. That's why one has to seize every opportunity when the weather's good, and this is one such opportunity. After a while, August calls out that he is hungry. I call back that he's the one responsible for the food.

He ambles up to the tent, happy and half-naked.

"You're the expedition chef, after all," I say. "It's not often that the expedition chef gets to make dinner in his underpants. Maybe it's happened before, but it's quite rare."

And then I tell him how important the chef was on earlier, historical expeditions, because what people ate had a big effect on how many physical obstacles they managed to overcome, and ultimately on the outcome of the entire expedition. I tell him about Norwegian explorer Fridtjof Nansen's polar expeditions, which I know he is interested in. I tell him about the American cowboys I enjoyed reading about when I was a boy. In magazines with names like *Silver Arrow*, I read stories in which the camp chef was often portrayed as fat and bearded with a rounded hat, its soft shape signaling that he wasn't all that tough. And maybe it's true that in the frontier days the chef was not always the first person to get shot through by the enemies, but I'm sure it happened more often than not.

August prepares pea soup. We eat until we're full and drink water drawn from The Nameless Lake. Our tent is nicely situated beneath a large pine, the line of drying clothes sways in the breeze, the sun beams, and small yellow mayflies bob across the surface of the lake from west to east. There's no sign of trout rising to eat them, but they are snatched up by swallows flying swift and low above the gleaming water.

We have one day's journey behind us, but much of this day still lies ahead. This fact worried me when I first began planning our expedition: that we would have too much time and too little to fill it with.

Might this idle time be too much?

Two adults can hike for an entire day. They can start in the early morning and go until late in the afternoon before they set up camp, eat dinner, and hit the hay. But this pacing is out of the question for a seven-year-old. On top of that, a seven-year-old expects the adult to have a plan, and at this very moment I have no plan.

August saves the day. He suggests that he will be my trainer and that I will be required to do all the exercises he instructs me to do. He proves to be a merciless trainer. I am made to do push-ups and sit-ups and a whole lineup of other activities that involves sticks and twigs as training implements, all of the exercises inspired by the film *Rocky IV*, which he has seen a clip of on YouTube without my permission. August is particularly fascinated by the scene in which Rocky is prepping for his encounter with the Russian boxing champion Ivan Drago by carrying logs and a bunch of other things one can find in the woods, and the moral of this scene is that those who use simple, natural methods are ultimately going to win over those who employ advanced technology.

August promotes himself to military instructor.

"You have to be as strong as the other daddies," he says, pushing me on.

When I tell him that I've done my very best but that I can't do anymore, he is mild and understanding and offers to massage my back and rub me down with sand from the lake, which he claims is good for the skin.

We whittle and fish and prepare more food. August plays for a long time inside the tent. I hum the "No more homework / No more clothes" song and jot down notes in my notebook.

It is evening.

It is night.

It is morning again.

◇◇◇

HAVE THE SKRIM MOUNTAINS CHANGED at all in the 122 years since a six-year-old boy got lost in them? Cabins have been built and the old farms have crumbled. Paths have been forged and cultural landscapes grown over. The tree line extends higher up the mountain than before. Predators have gone extinct. The golden eagle is still here, but the bear disappeared long ago.

The Skrim mountains have changed but less so than almost everything else around them. This landscape is still as original and untouched as anything in our times. The forests and waterways are the same. As are the mountains. They tower much as they did in Hans Torske's day and in the ten thousand years before that.

One can still walk for days in these mountains without encountering a single other human being.

◇◇◇

W E LEAVE THE CAMPSITE beside The Nameless Lake in
sunshine and under a lightly cloudy sky. Our path
veers upward. To the south the forest stretches as
far as the eye can see, a continuous green carpet broken
only by flecks of sparkling water. To the north are rocks of
every shape and color. In some places, the mountains are
steep and sharp. In others, they are rounded and smooth.
It's difficult to judge the distances and impossible to determine whether the terrain is flat and navigable all the way to
the peaks or whether gorges and ravines now hidden from
view will make for hard hiking.

We pause on the top of a ridge. Check the map while
nibbling energy bars and dried meat.

Few things are more pleasurable than studying a map,
dreaming yourself away, finding routes, making plans. You
unfold the map and stare at the contour lines and colors—
yellow, brown, green, blue; find a point some distance from
where you are; and try to imagine what it looks like there.
What might you expect to meet on the way, and how will
things look? It is a single stage of a small expedition, a
distance traveled in time and space, on a day of the calen-
dar year, through a landscape that, on this particular day,
appears a certain way.

The ridge is similar to the one we crossed the day before,
only it's at a higher altitude and the vegetation is thus

more sparse. There are no spruce trees here, only heather and dwarf birches. We are standing at the gateway to Skrim mountain itself. Enormous boulders are scattered across the terrain. I put one of them to use as a backrest.

Hardly anything grows here. Clinging to a small crack in the rock beside me are a few small white flowers with reddish stalks. I don't know what they're called—I don't know much about flowers—but they brighten up the barren landscape. In this light, the mountain is the opposite of the forest—exposed, unprotected, and with so much open space that the tiniest plants stand out against the naked bedrock, as if proclaiming: I am alive, right now. If you are a flower on a mountain, it's quite possible that you may live your entire life without anyone ever seeing you; but if someone does chance to pass, they cannot fail to take note.

August climbs on the boulders. I study the white flowers and think about Carl Linnæus, the Swedish botanist who gave the modern Latin names to all of our plants and whom we learned about at school. He lived during the Enlightenment. In his understanding, nature was a perfectly ordered system behind which stood the architect, God. Carl Linnæus viewed it as his task to map this divine system. No small task, but Linnæus did not suffer from a lack of confidence. He traveled the globe throughout his life and developed a system for classifying flora and fauna. He also wrote four autobiographies. Nowadays, someone like him would probably be diagnosed and medicated at an early age. But Linnæus took hold of his own life, or at least someone who realized his potential as a young man did. As I rest against the sun-warmed boulder, I picture the scene:

> Teacher: You down there, the one who can't sit still. What's your name again?
>
> Linnæus: Carl, sir.
>
> Teacher: Carl, right. This educational system does not suit you. You've got a good head, but clearly you can't sit still. So, I have a task for you. I want you to travel around Sweden cataloguing every botanical species that exists from Kiruna to Malmö. Maybe that will help channel your energy. It should also keep you busy for a while.

As I lean against the boulder thinking about Linnæus, I notice several large black birds farther up the mountain, hovering over something that is hidden behind the rocks and dwarf birches. The birds have found something and they are fighting over it. They screech. A dark, scraping sound, a kind of bark that echoes throughout the surrounding mountains, monotone, rhythmic, disquieting. I can hear more than see the ravens, but every so often one or more of them rises above the vegetation, floating on the air currents, and then dives again toward whatever it is they have found below.

"What are those birds called?" asks August.

"Ravens," I reply. "These birds haven't changed since the ice ages. In a sense, the same birds that were around back then are still around now. Their bodies are made up of a single color. Bills, feet, eyes, feathers—all of it black as coal. Ravens are smarter than any other animal or bird. If an animal is hurt, ravens can sense it, maybe even before the injured animal itself. They start to gather nearby, keeping watch over the animal, and at some point they realize that it is dying. That's when they start to hop closer, and then even closer, and finally they eat it. Maybe that's why our ancestors believed ravens were the messengers of death."

My monologue is interrupted by what only a few short days ago would have seemed unremarkable but now causes a minor sensation.

A human becomes visible over the hillcrest to the west.

It is a man. He is large and muscular and walks in a way that shows he's done this before. August and I stand and straighten our backs, the way you do when you are about to meet a very important person. The man gets closer. He doesn't stop when he reaches us; he merely slows his pace somewhat, says hi, and tells us that he is heading toward his car in the hope of getting there before a fierce rainstorm starts.

"It's going to cover the entire mountain range, and it will last for several hours, maybe even a day," the man says.

With that, he is off toward the forest in the south.

August and I stand looking at each other. A fierce rainstorm! What are we going to do? I don't think August is very worried about it. He doesn't tend to think about what is coming since it's not here yet.

I switch on my cell phone and check the weather forecast. The hiker is right. A large downpour is on the way; it will be directly overhead in only a few hours and it will indeed deck the entire mountain range with a thick layer of clouds and a deluge that does not look as if it is going to let up until the following day. There is no wind in the prediction, nor freezing temperatures, but there is a whole lot of water. And wherever there's a whole lot of water, you can be sure there will also be fog, which means no view, no perspective.

A hiker must always be prepared for rain. But knowing exactly what to do about it is another matter, especially when the only shelter you are carrying is a tiny tent and the landscape offers few options for cover.

It's one thing to get wet hiking when you know there's a cabin with a snug bed waiting for you at the end of the day. It's another thing entirely when you know that all you have is a tent. Yet very few people have actually experienced what this difference feels like in their body. If you know you'll be spending the night in a cabin, you can stay outside in inclement weather for as long as you want. It will feel like a walk in the park compared to sleeping in a sopping wet tent after you've gotten sopping wet on your hike.

Staying in a cabin is not very different from staying in an apartment in the city. If you go outside in the rain, you get wet and after that you go back inside, get warmed up, and put on dry clothes. Life in a cabin allows you to start each day fresh, dry, well fed and well rested after having slept in a warm, soft bed. Each morning you head out again, renewed and fully resourced to face the new day. In a tent, your body is slowly worn down by the elements, day by day. How quickly this happens depends on the terrain, and the weather, the worst of which is rain. When you're wet to the bone with no sign of the storm abating nor any shelter in which to dry off, tent life can rapidly take a heavy mental and physical toll. You start to long for home more than anything else.

There is a sense of gravity hovering over our current situation. August and I must do something, and quickly. I pore over the map and a plan starts to take shape. There's nothing to the north but a barren mountain, but to the southwest are mountain pastures with multiple farms. These are several hundred feet below our current elevation. The buildings are marked as small dark dots on the map. It's impossible to know what the buildings really look like or what state they are in, but the very fact that there are buildings is certainly alluring, even if it means we will have to deviate from our plan and walk in the opposite direction.

I call over to August that he should stop climbing. "We have to plot a new course," I say. I tell him about the farms and point at the map.

August imagines that we are going to get to sleep indoors, that we can sleep in beds and light a fire, and that maybe there will even be a kiosk where he can buy something.

I tell him that I seriously doubt this last part. We don't have a key to any of the buildings, and the map doesn't indicate the kind of places that are frequented by people. These buildings are miles and miles off the beaten track. They're probably shut and locked up, and we are most likely going to have to sleep outside.

But, I tell him, maybe there will be a porch on one of the buildings, a pile of boards, a shed, or something or other that we can sleep under to keep dry. It might not be perfect, but it will be a whole lot better than getting drenched out here in the open.

And so, it's decided. We note the direction and start hiking in our usual manner: he in front and me behind, a rhythmic march over the mountain.

The landscape through which we pass is boundless, clean and open, and infused with light. There's nothing to indicate a storm coming. Off to the west, layer upon layer of pine-covered hills lead inland toward Telemark county in shades of gray and I think: among the many human inclinations is this one, the urge to climb to the highest point and gaze out as far as the eye can see. This is something we strive for even without being aware of it. Here I'm not thinking of the kind of people who climb mountains just to take selfies bra-less, arms in the air, because these people have their own strange motives. It isn't so much mountain climbing that I'm thinking of as it is the human propensity to seek out a vantage point from which the eye may settle on a view that is far off, with no other motive than that it's meaningful to do so. Maybe it's the need for light, for perspective, as well as for distance. Or else the need to introduce an element of mystery and adventure into our rational minds and otherwise ordered existence. The faraway point toward which we gaze is real, but it is also unreal. The distant is alluring precisely because it is so far away—encapsulated in that special light that distance brings, that makes even the far-flung visible, and that orders the world in layers, like the layered shades of blue beyond blue beyond blue that are such a prevalent motif in classic works of Norwegian art. Maybe this need is deeply embedded within us from an era long past, remnants of the days when our ancestors wandered the savannahs of Africa. Maybe this desire for perspective comes from the same place as our love of sunsets.

We arrive at the highest part of the ridge. From here, we will turn south again and start our descent toward the pastures and the dark forests. For the first time, Styggemann peak becomes visible. It is the tallest massif towering above the rest of the mountain range, like a stranded whale, a dark colossus in granite. From our vantage point, the summit looks insurmountable, impossible to reach, which only increases my desire to set off for the top without delay. But the summit will have to wait. A rainstorm is coming. We have other matters more urgent now than mountaineering.

The path plunges steeply. After only a few yards, the expansive view is gone. Without a map and compass or a path as our guide, we could easily get lost in the forest. We might walk for days without once touching civilization or figuring out where we are.

The path is small and unmarked. Very few hikers, it seems, ever pass this way. I stay alert so we don't lose sight of it. It's easy to stop paying attention when you're walking, to allow your mind to wander off on thought trails that don't have anything to do with sticking to the path at hand, to turn left in front of a spruce tree because it looks like an opening, only to realize a few minutes later that you're lost.

The path is cushioned in blueberry shrubs and aging, grayish spruce trees. Insects hum and spidery threads gleam in the sunlight.

August chatters away. Whenever he's in the zone, he forgets all else. He babbles on merrily while plucking up objects along the path. He says something that makes him think of something else, which in turn makes him think of something else; he is a living stream of consciousness in the wilderness, enveloped in his own peculiar world, and I am certain that if I stopped him and said: "What is your name, where are you, where are we going? Answer me, quickly!" he would just stand there with his mouth agape and his eyes wide open, unable to answer.

Our path flattens out. The terrain opens up. We come to two old, weather-beaten farm buildings surrounded by lush meadows that once fed cattle in the summer months. This is a classic Norwegian landscape that grows wild and returns to forest if it is not maintained.

A creek flows in a dale at the edge of the meadow. August finds a frog swimming tenaciously against the strong current. He lifts it up carefully and starts to talk to it, just as I used to do at his age. Back then, every living thing was fascinating: everything that moved or crept was worth pausing for, to catch in my hands, lift up, examine.

I put my backpack down on the grass. Lie on my back and gaze up at the sky, listening to August's conversation with the frog. Above the treetops, the sky has turned gray. A change in the weather has snuck up on us, quietly and unremarkably. If we hadn't crossed paths with the other hiker, this shift in weather would have taken us by surprise.

A signpost informs us that this is private farmland and that tenting is not allowed. This upsets August, both because he is exhausted and would like to set up camp here, and because he is rattled that someone might dare to put up a sign telling other people that they don't have a right to be here in the middle of such a vast wilderness. August's voice has taken on a falsetto tone, and I know we need to put these two old farm buildings behind us as soon as possible and find some other options.

There are several paths leading in different directions. We choose the wrong one and have to turn around and retrace our steps. We choose another wrong one, and August hisses in exasperation. The third path leads to a meadow where there is one large main building and one smaller side building. Above the porch entrance to the main building is a large overhang. There's no one else in the meadow and, importantly, there's no sign forbidding campers.

We set up camp. Roll out our mats and sleeping bags on the porch, get out the Primus stove and food, drink a few quarts of water, and inspect our new accommodations. We stroll around the property, use the outhouse, and conduct the daily military training exercises. I don't think August realizes just how lucky we are to have found a solid roof over our heads to keep us dry when we go to sleep tonight or how demoralizing it might otherwise have been had we been forced to spend the following day hunched inside a clammy, wet tent.

We read Donald Duck comics and eat meat soup with no meat in it.

After that comes the rain.

◇◇◇

F OR THE NEXT FIFTEEN HOURS, it pours nonstop. The sky empties itself steadily; the cloud cover is a monotone shade of gray with no distinguishable lighter or darker flecks. No wind blows; there is nothing but a seemingly limitless deluge of water dropping from the sky.

August and I are seated beneath the porch overhang, peering out. The spruce trees that stand like stooping giants at one end of the meadow are almost invisible through the downpour. There is no longer any backdrop. There is only a gray wall of rain. Everything is wet. Even the sleeping bags and the Donald Duck comics have gotten damp in spite of the roof overhead.

I organize our backpacks.

August draws in his book.

Time passes slowly, as it should.

I tell August about the Second World War in Norway, about the heroes from Telemark, the famous Norwegian resistance group, probably both to remind myself and August that other people have been through worse times than we have. I tell him that in the winter of 1943 the heroes of Telemark hid out in a mountain region not very far away from Skrim, and that they ate nothing but reindeer moss for a whole winter. I notice the same expression on August's face that I have seen many times before, both on his and his friends' faces. It is the expression of someone concentrating all their energy on trying to imagine what it would be like to eat nothing but lichen for a whole winter.

"What do you remember from when I was little?" August asks me suddenly.

I must think before I reply.

"When you were little, I was always exhausted. We were always together, and yet I can hardly remember any of it. Whenever we look at pictures from the time you and Helena were little and I see myself in them, I always think: Is that me? Was I really there?

"A lot of things happened at once," I tell him. "We moved and renovated the house, and that's also when Grandma got sick and died only a few months later, and I was so stressed at work that I finally had to go on sick leave for several months. I was burned out, as we say, so instead of working I just pushed you around in your stroller through the city parks in Oslo. You would fall asleep in the stroller, but I knew that the moment I stopped pushing you, you would wake up. We walked past moms and dads seated on park benches, reading, with their babies asleep in their strollers beside them. It looked so peaceful, and I even remember that one dad had brought along a stainless steel thermos of coffee and was sitting on a bench drinking coffee and reading a thick novel. He seemed pretty confident that his baby was going to have a long nap. I wanted things to be like that too, so one time I brought along a book, and when we got to a park bench I stopped and sat down with the stroller beside me. But before I was able to read a single sentence, you started screaming and I had to get up and keep going. 'Can't you just sleep a little longer, can't you see that I'm burned out!' I thought. But you didn't see it; you always woke up if I stopped walking. You were already a type A person back then."

The evening comes quickly and the sky grows darker. The insects have vanished into the grass. The birds have stopped singing in the woods.

We read the final Donald Duck story we've brought along. Once we've finished it, we won't have any new comic book stories to divert us—or to block out nature. This Norwegian version of the original English comic book is issue number thirteen. The story features Mickey and Goofy. It's called "The Swamp Orchid" and it's about the two characters being sent out on behalf of the police chief because the next-to-last specimen of a rare orchid has been stolen from an exhibit in Duckburg. The thieves behind the crime are Blackbeard Pete and his gang, the Beagle Boys, and the last thing that happens is that Blackbeard Pete shoves Mickey into a bog of quicksand while yelling:

> *Since this is gonna be the last time we ever meet, I wanted to*
> *thank you for everything we've gone through together.*
> *Bye bye, Mickey Mouse!*
> *Ha, ha, ha!*

At the bottom of the page are the words: "To be continued in the next issue."

August has been through this before and it looks as though he has accepted his fate. We are in the middle of an isolated mountain landscape. He knows that the likelihood of coming across the next issue in the series is extremely low.

We continue talking. I am just about to tell him about Hans Torske, but then I hold back. It would be so fitting, here in this landscape that has not changed much since the year the young boy went astray, but I am worried that August will misinterpret the story as a kind of foreshadowing for what lies ahead. We manage to amuse ourselves beneath the porch overhang, in spite of our thirty-eight-year age difference. August's presence is reassuring. He is not only my son, he is my friend, a mercurial individual given to unpredictable whims, but a friend nonetheless.

Soon it is night. August tells me about his buddies and his class and his school. I tell him about my grandfather Erling, his great-grandfather, who almost exclusively ate waffles in the final years of his life. In the beginning, he would eat waffles made from waffle batter. But then he realized that the waffle iron could cook fluids of any kind, and with that he began to expand his definition of waffles until, finally, the combined ingredients could be just about anything. Visits to Grandpa thus became a gastronomical challenge for everyone but him.

August likes it when I talk about Grandpa Erling. Still, there is a limit to how long anyone can stay under a porch overhang in a meadow in the middle of a forest, and at some point his patience wears thin.

"Why are we here?" August asks, his voice almost a sob.

"Because it's raining," I say. "We don't have a choice. This is the best place we could possibly be."

August is struggling internally. He knows what I mean, and he also knows I'm right. But he doesn't want to stay here any longer, and I can fully empathize. I bring out every distraction I can think of but nothing helps. Every now and then he might forget about our unfortunate situation briefly, but that moment doesn't last long.

I pull out the map. My brain is spinning with various solutions. Our plan was to continue west for another day or two and after that to summit Styggemann from the northwest. But now it occurs to me that there might be another way to head directly to the mountain tomorrow. I have been fixated on the original plan, clinging to it, but there's no one forcing us to follow it in exactly that way or forbidding us from taking a different course. We are at liberty to decide for ourselves—this is after all the premise for our little expedition—and I happen to know that a path leads straight toward the top of Styggemann from the very meadow in which we find ourselves now. The path is perhaps steeper than other routes, but I've hiked it before and I think August can handle it.

I tell him, "If the sun comes out tomorrow, let's hike to the top of Styggemann."

August lights up. He needs something concrete to hold on to in all of this idle waiting, and there are few things as concrete as a mountaintop.

I explain the plan. Once we get to the top, we will have reached our goal. From there, we will turn south and east but we won't go back to the car the same way we came. Instead we will continue across a mountain range that is lower than Styggemann but even more barren, so barren that there aren't any paths at all, only boggy marshes and flat ridges. The going will be as hard as it was to get here and up to Styggemann, maybe even harder. I don't know how long it will take us to cross this mountain range, but that will be the start of our homeward journey.

August grants his approval of the plan. The idea that we will start our return journey to the car after summiting Styggemann is an uplifting thought that gives him an extra push of motivation before he finally falls asleep.

I lie awake in my sleeping bag next to him. I am reading a book by John Muir, an iconic figure in American natural history. He catalogued the flora in the mountains of California in the last half of the 1800s, not unlike what Carl Linnæus did in Sweden almost one hundred years earlier. Muir spent much of his life in the Sierra Nevada mountains and was directly involved in founding one of the United States' most famous national parks, Yosemite, in 1890.

Above our heads, a large spider dangles on a thread. With its macabre, almost futuristic appearance and mechanical movements, it is the incarnation of everything we think of as revolting in this world. Maybe it will belay itself down under the cover of nightfall and creep across our faces or slowly down into our sleeping bags. I am tempted to smash it with a rolled-up Donald Duck comic, but I just finished reading a sentence in John Muir's book that keeps me from doing so. On one of his treks through the mountains of

California, Muir wrote down the names of all the trees and flowers and plants with unflagging thoroughness. He drew them in his sketch pad and described their appearance and characteristics, but he was much more than a simple scientist. He was also someone who experienced a strong sense of interdependence with the natural world, with untouched landscapes, and who recognized the innate value of nature.

He wrote this about poisonous plants:

> Like most other things not apparently useful to man, it has few friends, and the blind question, "Why was it made?" goes on and on with never a guess that first of all it might have been made for itself.

I leave the spider to its own diversions and try turning my thoughts to something else. I read John Muir's book. I jot down thoughts both big and small in my journal. Finally, I switch off my headlamp and fall sleep.

I wake up throughout the night. Every time I open my eyes, I see a tiny brown field mouse perched on the flagstone nearby. It moves silently, sniffing its way ahead in the twilight with its long whiskers and great black eyes. It sits up on its hind legs and tries to open our food container. I don't try to stop it; I know the container is too difficult for a field mouse to open. The mouse is mere inches away from an enormous cache of rich, tasty food inside the container. And yet it is very far away from these riches, but I am the only one of us who knows it.

There is another thing we should understand when small children get lost. They will almost always head uphill. If they reach the top of a hill or ridge, they will then follow it until they arrive at a new hill to walk up. It's as if they do not have the heart to leave the hill untried. Maybe this has to do with the feeling of emptiness that stretches out in front of the body? Maybe it gives them a feeling of safety, of being close to the earth, every time the mountain rises up in front of them.

—Leif Halvorsen, *Yearbook, 1967*, Drammens and Opland's Tourist Association

◇◇◇

WHERE DID HANS TORSKE GO on the day he vanished from Breistul pasture, and why didn't the search party find him?

He did not go north across the flat agricultural landscape, nor did he go west toward the river. He didn't head south, over Breistulknatten mountain. That way is too steep; it juts straight up behind the farmhouses and so this was not the direction he chose. These days a thick evergreen forest extends up a good portion of the mountainside, but in Hans Torske's day the forest had been clear-cut. If he had chosen that way, he could have at any moment turned around to see the farmhouse roofs behind him. In which case he would easily have found his way back.

I believe Hans Torske lost his way in the forest that grew up alongside the farm. This forest is not far away; it is only a dozen yards off to the side of the buildings. But the woods here are dark and dense. It was into this space that he wandered, and at some point he must have stopped and looked around and realized that he was somewhere he'd never set foot before. He tried finding his way back again, but he had been so lost in thought as he made his way into the forest that he hadn't paid any attention to where he was going or what direction he came from. The nature of a forest is that it keeps you from walking in a straight line.

Hans Torske must have veered back and forth between the trees, the way children often do, and thus it's likely that he had already gotten lost shortly after entering the forest.

If he had been lucky and chosen the right direction, Hans Torske would have emerged from the forested area in no time. But he did not. Instead, he wandered eastward along the foot of the mountains. If from here he had gone straight up the side of Breistulknatten mountain, he would have been able to look out over the farms. There's an additional factor that could also have guaranteed a safe return: the slope of the ground. If Hans Torske had been able to remember that he'd walked uphill into the forest, he could perhaps have figured out that to get back home he needed to walk downhill. But if he had instead headed east, as I suspect, the first part of the terrain is relatively flat and there is no uphill or downhill slope to help determine the direction. I believe this is the most important reason why he never found his way home again.

I, too, have walked through this terrain. I've stood in Breistul pasture looking out in every direction, just as the boy's mother and the search party must have done. I understand why they first thought to search along the river. It runs alongside the farm, water is alluring to small children, and a river poses an acute threat to young lives.

Hans Torske never went west toward the river. He walked in the opposite direction, and in the time it took the search party to comb the riverbanks, he was able to wander farther and farther away. There are several farms along his chosen path. These farms must have been populated at the time because the farmers here were among the first community members to respond to the call for help.

Hans Torske must have passed very close to these farms, but without seeing them. The forest is dense, and it's quite possible one might not even see a building that is very close by. There can be no other explanation, for at this point the boy must have understood that he was lost. He must have been scared, and if he had seen a building he would most certainly have made his way toward it.

But he did not see any buildings, and after having passed them, there were no more buildings, at least not where he headed after that.

It is at this point that Hans Torske began to walk uphill. He turned south and continued on an incline in one of two ravines that slice through the landscape. The ravines run parallel to each other from northeast to southwest. On the north side, Breistulknatten mountain shoots almost straight into the sky. To the south, the other mountains veer up steeply toward the Styggemann and Skrim peaks. The terrain is craggy and difficult to navigate and a hiker's energy is quickly depleted. At the base of the northernmost ravine is a marked path. From there, you get a good view of just how steep the south side of Breistulknatten mountain is, a gray, nearly vertical surface that plunges 100 to 150 feet from the summit to the forest below.

The southern ravine is separated from the northern one by a low wooded ridge. This ravine is narrower and darker and contains no indication of human travel. A small stream runs along its base, carrying clear, cold water from the mountain. My theory is that this is where Hans Torske walked. He probably discovered the stream at the foot of the mountain, not far from the farm. And then he followed it up because the stream, babbling and alive, stood out in the homogenous forest. Had he followed it downstream, it would have led him back to the pasture and the farms. But instead he followed it up, toward the south, and it brought him deeper and deeper into the mountains.

What happened next depends on two conditions that are closely related: weather and temperature. If conditions were mild and clear, Hans Torske may have been able to survive for several days, perhaps even weeks. But if it was rainy and cold, his life would have been endangered in mere hours.

Facts support the first theory. The Norwegian Meteorological Institute was already making daily measurements at the time when Hans Torske vanished. These measurements were not as precise as they are nowadays, and there were fewer measuring stations. Still, a measuring station was located not far from Kongsberg, and its records for that day in July 1894 indicate a steady high-pressure system across the region that had been there for quite some time. The temperature recorded on the day of Hans Torske's disappearance was seventy degrees Fahrenheit. There was neither wind nor rain. It was a warm, pleasant summer afternoon, the kind of day where you can walk around in light clothing until late in the evening.

It was under such favorable conditions that Hans Torske followed the course of the stream upward until he reached the high mountain plateau. From there he had a good view in several directions, but perhaps he arrived in the middle of the night and didn't see the view—or maybe he saw the view and the landscape but was only more confused by it. Maybe he had never been on a high mountain plateau before, in such a strange landscape that was so different from the familiar city streets of his hometown.

He got lost and wandered farther and farther into the wilderness, traversing great distances, first here and then there without even realizing it. He was able to cover more distance than the search party would have thought possible for a six-year-old child. Perhaps he looked for the tallest peak in order to climb up and get some perspective. Perhaps at some point he even stood on the summit of Styggemann. There is a small stone hut on the highest spot nowadays and it would have been a natural point toward which to navigate, but in his day there would have been no such hut. The building was first erected in 1927 and registered to the owner of the forest as a lookout post for fires.

In 1894, no humans had settled in the Skrim mountains. There were, however, bears, golden eagles, and wolves. Skrim was a merciless wilderness, and no one passed through it without having a good reason to do so, most often because their work required it. Cutting down trees, picking berries, fishing, or hunting. People back then did not go swimming in their leisure time. They didn't view nature as an arena for recreation; they knew it only as a workplace.

Hans Torske would have found water to drink in several spots but there is little to eat in these mountains at the beginning of July. A few berries, perhaps, but berries don't provide a small body with much energy. In a few short days he would have grown emaciated. His organs would slowly have begun to fail. His body would have prioritized blood flow to its most vital organs, his heart and brain. His kidneys would have stopped working, leading to an accumulation of toxins in the body, which would slowly have shut down more and more functions.

There is a possibility that this is indeed what happened to Hans Torske following his disappearance. There is, however, another possibility.

A steady high-pressure system and hot temperatures in the summertime often result in sudden and severe weather changes. Thunderstorms are characterized not only by electrical discharges into the atmosphere but also by abruptly decreasing temperatures and large, localized downpours. Thunder and lightning would frighten any small boy who is alone in a dark forest. Large deluges can cause steam and fog, which reduce visibility. Details from the meteorological institute show that just such a thunderstorm occurred in the region of Christiania (what is modern-day Oslo) in the days before Hans Torske vanished. What if the weather system had pushed south toward Kongsberg?

If that is the case, the story about the boy in the Skrim mountains becomes a different tale altogether.

We must go back to the point when Hans Torske comes across the stream that runs toward the southernmost of the two ravines leading up toward the high mountain plateau. He follows the stream, but at some point he leaves it and begins to walk up the mountainside heading east. The slope quickly becomes steeper, so steep that a boy of six would have to crawl on his hands and feet to continue. If Hans Torske continues to the top, he has reached a mountain that is hundreds of feet below Styggemann. The mountain is rugged and scarred with fissures. It is closed in by an impenetrable thicket of stiff, dense dwarf birch trees. Picking one's way through such a landscape is exhausting work.

Hans Torske follows the mountain east. First up, and then down again. At the foot of the mountain is a large bog that stretches from the northernmost edge of the mountain range all the way south toward the foot of Styggemann. If Hans Torske is overtaken by a sudden rainstorm and plummeting temperatures, it is likely that he has walked directly to this spot. He may have reached the summit on the night of his disappearance, or the next morning, cold and wet and weak, worn out from all the hours spent picking his way through the relentless terrain.

He may have become sick and feverish.

He may not have noticed his body temperature falling.

It is possible for a human to freeze to death in a Norwegian forest in the middle of summer. It's not unusual for the temperatures here to drop below fifty degrees, which is much lower than the temperature of a human body.

One way of cooling down is called mild hypothermia. You don't get frostbite as you would in the winter when temperatures are freezing cold. There's no drama in the situation and one does not experience it as acutely. When the reduction of temperature takes place so slowly, the body adjusts to it by degrees. Cells reduce their activities. Metabolism slows down and the body enters a state of hibernation. You feel drowsy and lose your sense of reality. You lie down and fall asleep. From the sleep state, you pass into a delirious, comatose condition, and if help is not forthcoming, there's little to prevent the body from slowing down completely and the heartbeat from stopping. At this point, the heart isn't getting enough oxygen from the cells to continue its work.

It is possible that Hans Torske may have wandered through the Skrim mountain landscape in pleasant summer conditions, but it's also possible he may have been surprised by untimely bad weather. I don't know which of these possibilities is more likely, nor will we ever have a definitive answer. But regardless of which story I choose to believe, a single fact remains: at one point or another, this young boy stood on the vast bogland below Styggemann, looking out across the landscape toward the north.

Of the vanished child there has, as yet, been no trace found.
(...) All hope is not lost, however, of finding the child alive.
Other examples exist of children from this city having van-
ished and being found again after three days in relatively good
health. We wish to encourage the city's populace to continue
assisting the parents in their search for the child, and not to
give up as long as there is still hope of finding him.

—*Kongsberg Adresse* (newspaper), July 14, 1984

◇◇◇

A BOY WALKS ALONE through the vast landscape. Hundreds of people are searching for him: his mother and father, and many others. They are not far away, but the boy does not know this as he walks. Soon it is dusk, soon it is night, soon it is morning again.

The boy continues.

One day passes, two days, three days.

Or perhaps only mere hours pass.

No one knows, and no one will ever know. Only the boy knows, and he can no longer tell us.

But one thing is certain.

He stands on a bog, gazing north. He looks out over the landscape beneath the mountain, down in the valley where the farm meadow is, the place he left. From here he can see farms and fields, and farther away, to the east, his hometown.

He sees all of this, and he must think, *That's where I live, down there, that's where I have to go.* But he doesn't go, he never goes down. He stands there, perhaps in the middle of the night, unable to glimpse his hometown in the darkness; or maybe it is rainy or foggy with zero visibility. Maybe he thinks that if he can see them, they must be able to see him.

I'll wait here. They are going to come get me soon.

At the edge of the bog is a large stone. He walks over to the stone and can feel its warmth. This is a good place to rest until he feels stronger again. He puts his hat under his head. He takes off his jacket and spreads it over himself. He falls asleep on the stone in the middle of the vast, barren landscape.

◇◇◇

I WAKE TO THE SOUND of falling drops, not several all at once, but one single drop after another. Each drop makes the same sound as it hits the ground and they follow at steady intervals.

Plop ... plop ... plop ... plop.

I open my eyes. At first I don't remember where I am. Then it comes back to me. On Skrim. Beneath a porch overhang. With August. The rainstorm yesterday, that is why we are here.

The brown field mouse is gone. August is burrowed somewhere deep inside his sleeping bag, and outside the sun is shining. I fall asleep again to the sound of drops falling, rhythmically, one by one.

August shakes me awake. There is a flushed grin across his face. He is in a better mood now than when he fell asleep. A true type A specimen.

A buoyant, nearly euphoric air hovers over our breakfast and obligatory morning military drills. The sky is blue, there is no wind. It is the perfect day to climb a mountain. We pack our gear and are soon retracing our steps. The plan is to head up the steep slope through the thick forest, up to the mountain plateau where we first met the other hiker. And from there, to turn toward Styggemann.

We pass the two farmhouses with the camping-prohibited signs. Each of us thinks our own thoughts about this incessant human propensity to own something and to keep everyone else away from it. We enter the woods. Our boots make sucking noises as we lift them from the sopping forest floor. Around us, everything trickles and flows and runs. The light refracts in the water droplets on the conifer needles, it twinkles on spiderwebs. A tiny bird sings from a fir tree whose branches are bedecked with long, grayish tree moss, and its melody is one solitary, mournful piping tone followed by another. I think it is a bullfinch.

Where the forest floor is scraggier, the water flows in even streams over the ground. The grass bends beneath the weight of the droplets, and in the shadowy coolness of the undergrowth the air is so saturated with oxygen that it feels like we are re-experiencing the creation story.

August walks ahead.

I follow behind.

Neither of us speaks.

My pack feels heavier today, even if it's not. I was initially worried about whether I would be able to carry such a heavy pack over the distance we have already covered. I can feel the strain in my shoulders, and in my back. There's not enough time for my body to recover from one day to the next, and on this day I have to carry the backpack up hundreds of feet of steep elevation.

August appears to carry his backpack with ease even if it is, relatively speaking, just as heavy for him as mine is for me.

After a few hours, we are above the spruce forest. We once again see Styggemann looming to the northeast, standing out against the sky like a heavily armored, prehistoric crustacean.

"Is that where we're going?" August asks.

"Yes," I reply, "that's Styggemann."

What he doesn't yet know is that the way there is much rougher than it looks from where we stand. The path first drops down into a dark glen before climbing steeply toward the top. It is typical of this particular mountain range that no one type of terrain dominates for too long; each is broken up by other variations, as if the landscapes are fighting over which of them gets to achieve total dominion.

Just how far a person is able to walk over the course of a day depends more upon the kind of terrain than on the person doing the walking. Many trails seem extraordinarily hospitable for hikers. On the Hardanger Plateau, for instance, a person can walk for entire days across a landscape that is as flat and accommodating as any wide-open boulevard in a French city. Because this terrain is so high up, where snow runoff originates, the plateau itself is surprisingly dry.

In other regions, such as Norway's Femundsmarka, which comprises forests, lakes, and marshes, hikers can experience both hospitable and inhospitable trails. In the Rondane mountains (the oldest national park in Norway), hikers are often surprised to come across accumulations of enormous round stones, boulder fields from ancient times.

It can take hours to cross these stone fields, and one wrong step with a heavy backpack can result in a sprained foot or broken ankle. Among other mountain ranges, for example in the northwest of Norway, the terrain can be extremely craggy, which is why the question about elevation is so important when judging distances and creating a day-by-day plan for the trip.

An adult carrying a full backpack travels through average terrain at a pace of about 1.8 miles per hour. If you add ten minutes of rest per hour, plus one hour for a more extensive lunch-and-rest break, this means that an adult could walk between seven and ten miles on an average day.

I don't know how far it is to the top of Styggemann. It is less important than the fact that we will first have to hike down quite far and then, directly after that, straight up. Add to that the fact that walking down into the bottom of a glen means heading in the same direction as all of the water from last night's downpour.

The mountain plateau is scattered with some remaining boulders. We take off our packs and lean them up against one of the stones. If Styggemann is a troll, these enormous rocks must be an amusement for him: small granite marbles that he has tossed about in some kind of pattern, like a type of prehistoric bocce. We sip fresh water and eat chocolate and crispbread spread with cheese from a tube (a favorite among Norwegian spreads, this one is flavored like ham). August entertains himself by gathering small, flat stones covered in yellow and green map lichens and throwing them as far as he can, down into the forest below. He lobs them down the mountain, and from below you can hear a hollow sound, as if there's a room there that no one knows about. These rocks have perhaps been lying here unmoved for ten thousand years. Until a seven-year-old boy from Oslo comes ambling by, and all of a sudden the rocks are flying through the air before landing deep within a dense undergrowth of grass and moss and ferns.

"Do you realize that you are throwing those stones into a totally different world?" I ask.

August stares at me without responding. Maybe he thinks I'm crazy. Maybe he thinks I'm only joking. More likely he doesn't hear what I'm saying because he is so occupied by seeing how far he can throw the rocks, and what happens when they land. This activity is on par with gathering sticks, and as such it holds great appeal for children in every country, in every era, in every culture.

The stones may as well have been loaded onto a ship headed to the Caribbean—that's how different conditions are in the forest below. They have been lying in open mountain terrain, becoming the kind of stones that belong in an alpine setting, stones that are almost always covered in lichen. But map lichen only thrives in high-elevation settings such as this; it won't be able to survive in the lower-elevation forest below and so the stones will slowly shift in appearance. The map lichen will die away over time and green biomass or a thick, soft kind of moss will cover the stones instead—at least until some other boy chances past and tosses them back up onto the high mountain, and then the entire process will start again. Anyone who has found such a stone high in the mountains has experienced this: the lichen on the alpine stone you brought home to adorn your entryway gradually disappears and the stone slowly becomes just another average rock.

"Is it time to go yet?" August yells.

He wants to keep going. He is brimming with enthusiasm now that the goal is in sight. We are here, and up there is Styggemann, and to get to the top we have to start hiking again. It's as simple as that.

I nod in affirmation. "Put your backpack back on. You go on ahead, but pay attention that we don't lose the trail because it's easy to get lost in the terrain we're entering now. We're going to lose the view, the only fixed point we've had, and if we lose the trail too we won't have anything to navigate by but the slope. To the west of us, it goes downhill the whole way. To the east, it goes uphill. We will be on the edge of the slope, so we'll have the uphill on our right side and the downhill on our left. We should also pay attention to the water flow. When the water slows down and makes big, flat puddles, that's how we'll know we've reached the bottom of the glen. That's when the climb will start. From there we should see a stream coming from the north, down from the lakes under Styggemann. We'll follow the stream up toward the top."

We hike for half an hour with the sun at our backs. And then we begin the descent. The forest closes in behind us like a zipper. The earth is saturated with water. Black soil sticks to our boots. The moisture lining the grass makes our pants stick to our legs. August slips on a rock and falls forward, so that his backpack hits him in the back of his head. He gets up and curses his backpack.

"Stupid shit," he says. "Fuck, hell, damn!"

We continue.

I deliberately don't mention his swearing.

August slips again.

I can tell he is having a difficult time.

The dense deciduous forest gives way to an old spruce forest. The forest floor is more spacious beneath these trees. Nothing grows here but those low green plants that one easily associates with creation, and from which, by some art or design, we ourselves originate. It's like diving under water, like swimming over a seafloor covered by seagrass. It is dark like twilight, murky, and quiet. The scattered bird sounds amplify the silence. We are somewhere outside of the world, in a place of utter calm, left to itself and to the shifts of the passing years.

August stops. I can tell something is wrong.

"Are you hungry, thirsty, too hot, too cold?" I ask.

"Yes, Daddy! I am!" he answers.

He is too hot. I suggest he take off both his shell and fleece jacket so he's only wearing his thin wool sweater. That seems to help.

We descend deeper and deeper into the glen.

August slips and falls. Just before he loses his footing, I foresee what is going to happen. He grabs hold of a half-rotten stick in the middle of the path. He places his foot in such a way that I know he is going to slip, and then he does.

He falls down and stays there.

This is like that moment in cross-country skiing when the skier is already stiff, when their only hope of continuing to their goal is to maintain a mechanical rhythm, to repeat the same motions over and over again without deviating from that pattern no matter what, to trick the body into forgetting that it is completely worn out. But when one of the skis slips on an uphill, the skier has to maneuver their body unexpectedly, the muscles have to compensate for the imbalance, and this additional movement outside of the rhythm is the skier's downfall. It's only yards later, when their body stiffens up, that the skier realizes all of their energy has been spent, that they won't be able to pick up the pattern again, and from that point on, all is lost.

August pulls himself back up and keeps going.

For the first time on our expedition, I can hear that he is crying, painful sobs originating from deep down in his belly that may have come regardless of the situation. He walks and sobs, walks and sobs. When we finally reach the bottom and the terrain flattens out, he stops.

He sinks to the ground and says: "Why, Daddy? Why did you bring me with you?"

I sit down beside him. We are seated beside the ruins of an ancient dwelling site. In the 1600s, summer farm buildings were erected here. Now almost nothing is left but these ruins; the rest has returned to the soil, swallowed by the earth and moss and mushrooms and lichen. Nature tears everything to pieces, breaks it down and transforms it into food for new life, returning it to its natural state again over time. Even a house where someone once lived.

"I want to go home," August says.

I don't know what to say. I feel mean and dumb. I ask if he'd like to sit on my lap. He would, and then he cries even harder.

In the dark half-light of the glen, a deep whimpering sound emanates from a source that has been filling up gradually, a cry that would most likely have come out at some time or another and so it may as well come now, at the bottom of a glen beneath Styggemann.

"I like expeditions, I like to go hiking. But I miss people," August says.

I've understood this for quite a while now; this fact was apparent from the first day of our hike. When August accompanied me on his very first camping trip years ago, he was four. Back then, his primary challenge was walking. The fact that it was only the two of us wasn't a problem at the time because his world didn't extend much farther than that. These days however, the problem isn't so much the physical as the psychological challenge. The challenge of being alone for days on end with no one else to talk to but me, torn away from the members of his daily support network, all of the routines that give order to his existence, and the surroundings that are safe and familiar. I am his father, a person who fulfills several important functions in his life, but I'm not everything.

"I miss people," August repeats.

His cries grow louder and louder and I don't know what to say. I revert to a trick I've used before, and that is to start talking about a popular Norwegian adventure TV series from the 1970s about the Dal brothers and Professor Drøvel and all of the magical doors that appear along the shoreline of a river. August has watched the series several times and he loved the episode about the secret doors: that in the middle of the wilderness there might be doors that you could walk through and be transported to an entirely different place.

He perks up and says that if there was a door like that here, he wishes it would lead directly to Ullevaal Stadium, the Norwegian national soccer stadium that is also our local shopping mall. If there were such a door, we could walk through it this very moment and go straight over to Burger King before transporting back and continuing our hike to Styggemann.

I tell August I can carry his backpack to the top. He likes this suggestion. I take out some food. August changes into shorts and a T-shirt. He wants to know if the Dal brothers—Gaus, Roms, and Brumund—are still alive. I tell him that Gaus and Roms are alive, but that Brumund is dead.

"Brumund's real name is Trond Kirkvaag, and he died from cancer a few years before Grandma," I explain to him. "They were about the same age when they died, only a little over sixty."

"And Prince," August adds, referring to the American music artist who died just a few months ago.

At this point, I realize that he has gotten over the reason why we are sitting here in the first place: his despondency at finding himself alone with no one but his father in the middle of the wilderness.

August wipes his tears and stands up. He continues talking about Prince and the Dal brothers while I stuff our things back into the backpacks. I place his pack on top of mine and strap them together. I take his jacket and fleece and tie them to the straps on the outside of my pack so that now the only thing he has to carry is himself. I lift the backpack onto my back. Just heaving it onto my shoulders and then standing up is a near-impossible feat. This back-pack combination weighs between seventy-five and ninety pounds.

August is as light as a feather. He vanishes in the thick undergrowth. I call out that he has to wait for me. The path is so faint I'm worried about losing him. I call out again, but there's no reply. If he continues for a hundred yards in the wrong direction, he will soon be too far away to hear me. Sound doesn't travel far in terrain like this. There's almost zero visibility. If he walks for another hun-dred yards in the wrong direction, he'll be even more lost, and this is how it happens, how a person can get lost in less than a half hour.

I call out again, and a few seconds later he pops up in an opening in the shrubbery above me, cheerful and energetic, skipping, and restless to reach the top.

I think he is relishing the new situation. That now I am the one dragging along while he feels fit and ready to face big challenges. I admonish him that it's extra important now that we don't lose sight of one another. August seems to understand that I'm serious. He continues along ahead of me, but at a slower pace.

The hiking poles help. Two arms and a thigh are only barely able to lift the combination of human and backpacks up and up, one single step at a time. August appears unaffected by the elevation gain. Children are much stronger than adults if you measure their strength in relation to their body weight, which can be evidenced by taking them to the nearest climbing wall. They will almost always master climbing better than adults, in part because they are nimbler, but also, and primarily, because they have much more strength in relation to their body weight. August and I have discussed this idea several times, among others while bouldering in one of Oslo's many climbing gyms. And we have discussed it at our summer cabin, when we've watched ants carrying other insects across the bedrock. An ant can easily carry another ant, and in a manner that would be impossible for a human to replicate.

When he was younger, August loved that I would ask him this rhetorical question to which he already knew the answer: "In relation to its own body weight, which creature do you think is the strongest in the world?"

"Ant!"

And then I would have to tell him that if ants were as big as humans, they would rule the world, and the rest of us would be in trouble.

We reach a plateau with a small tarn in the middle of a bog. I tell August we need to take a break. We have to fill up our water bottles, as this is likely the last water source before the top.

A great tit is perched on a dwarf birch nearby. The bird is pecking away frenetically at something, a bud or an insect. Maybe it's hungry. Maybe it's pecking simply to pass the time.

A great tit that is pecking at an insect on a dwarf birch tree does not have any thoughts about what it is doing, who it was yesterday, or what it will do tomorrow. It doesn't even have a concept of itself and its place in the world, and maybe this is the characteristic that most distinguishes humans from animals. We have an ego. We can picture ourselves from the outside, evaluate our actions and habits, and use our free will to choose to change. Our conscious will offers us choice, and with choices come dilemmas. We have the ability to choose for the good of ourselves and others, but we also have the capacity to choose destruction. For the great tit, life is simple. It doesn't have a single choice to make, nor can it be blamed for the results.

August sits in the heather. He is digging with a stick in the soft bog. He appears consumed by this activity. I don't know what it is he hopes to accomplish, and I don't even know if he knows. I ask if he thinks life is simple or hard. I have to repeat the question three times before he lifts his head.

"Do you think life is simple or hard?" I ask.

"Simple," answers August and keeps digging.

◇◇◇

W E LINGER AT THE LAKE. To the west we are able to look out far over Telemark county. Layer after layer of forest-clad ridges, seemingly devoid of color from where we sit. The closest ridges have a dark, almost charcoal hue, and each subsequent range behind them has a slightly paler, gray shade.

From here, we have a clear view to the northeast of the top of Styggemann and the small stone hut at the summit. As with all famous mountains—either world famous because they are global landmarks or locally famous because they are landmarks within a particular geographical area—Styggemann is steeped in legends and stories about the mountain's origins. Creation stories that emerged once, very long ago, in an era when people knew less about how the world was formed but because of this had more vivid imaginations and perhaps more need for stories to explain certain natural events and peculiar landscapes.

Lightning and thunder.

Frost and flood.

Drought and wildfires.

Every explanation was a reference to something secular or religious, with mythical roots.

Styggemann has its own legend. The story goes that there was once a troll living in these parts, and this troll did not like people coming around. The troll lived on top of the mountain, from where he had a good view of trespassers. If he saw humans, he threw huge stones at them—large, angular boulders like the ones that August climbed on earlier. According to this story, the existence of the troll is the reason these boulders are scattered across the terrain. The modern explanation points to the ice ages. The troll only ventured outside when the sky was overcast, but one day the sun came out unexpectedly and the troll didn't have time to hide. The legend about Styggemann of the Skrim mountains thus has the same ending as almost every other story of its kind: the troll turned to stone.

Even today, you can make out the contours of the troll's face at the top of Styggemann. To see this profile, you must stand at a specific spot in relation to the mountain. I don't think we are at that spot right now, and I certainly cannot make out anything face-like. But I know that to see the face, you have to tilt your head to the left. Then you will see, if you are particularly inclined to see it, a face etched into the mountain. The face is staring up at the sky. It is the face of a creature lying on its back. A crack in the mountain makes the eyes, and a bulging crag is the nose. A steep crevice is the mouth. I have seen photos of this face in books. The creature reminds me of the moai stone statues on Easter Island. It is not actually ugly, as the name Styggemann implies (*stygg* means "ugly" in Norwegian). It does not look angry. Rather, it appears somewhat mild and amazed. But it must be a troll, and this is the thing about most Norwegian mountains. There are stories and legends about almost every single mountain in my country, and a remarkable number of them got their start as trolls.

I tell August the legend. I ask if he can see the face of the troll in the mountain.

"There is the nose, there are the eyes—the troll's eyes are pretty small—and there is his chin. He looks like Voldemort," he says after two seconds' thought.

The last stage to the top is like the final sprint, and August likes final sprints. He is in his element. He dashes off once again, and once again I call him back. We have to start climbing now, up a mountainside with steep downhill drops. There are even cliffs in places, and I don't want him to fall off.

When there are only a few yards left to the top, I allow him to finish at his own pace. I crawl the last steps on all fours, and when I lift my head above the final rock edge to the summit, I see him sitting happily on the top, beaming at me.

I sink down next to August and place an arm around his shoulder. It is the afternoon. It's taken us an entire day to get here. We are drenched with sweat. We are so high up that it feels like we are looking lengthwise along the bottom of the clouds and not up at them. Off in the distance, we can see the Lifjell and Blefjell and Gaustatoppen mountains and the city of Kongsberg. We see places we don't know the names of.

I point at the boggy region to the northwest. It is only a few hundred yards below the summit, no more than half a mile as the bird flies. Between the bogs and us are several small lakes. The bogs are yellowish orange and vast. They are surrounded by gnarled dwarf birches and covered by cloudberry shrubs and a white carpet of cotton grass, or what we call *myrull* (bog wool) in Norwegian.

I have often wanted to tell August the story about Hans Torske. I was tempted on our first night in the tent, and again when we sat by The Nameless Lake, when we were together beneath the porch overhang in the rain, and when we rested at the bottom of the glen. Each time I decided against it, but now that we are here, seated on top of the world beneath a bright summer sky with the warmth of the sun on our faces, it's hard to imagine any other ending than this one.

"Once a little boy about your age was walking around down there," I say, pointing at the bog below us. "He had gotten lost. He was all by himself, with no food or warm clothes or any adults to help him."

"What was his name?" asks August.

"His name was Hans Torske," I tell him. "He lived over a hundred years ago."

I tell him the story about the boy who got lost.

When I finish, August says: "What happened? Did he find his way back home? Did the adults find him? What happened to that boy?"

The boy who vanished over one year ago has been found.

—*Kongsberg Adresse* (newspaper), July 31, 1895

◇◇◇

I‎T IS LATE SUMMER; the year is 1895. One year has passed
since Hans Torske disappeared from the farm and people
are no longer looking for him. They must have given up
at some point, first the search party, and then the people
from the surrounding farms, and finally his mother and
father and older brother, Erik. As the summer turned to
autumn and the autumn to winter, their last hope was
extinguished. It gets very cold on Skrim. The first snows
fall in October.

It is one of the last days of July, and the late summer has
already left its mark on the wilderness. Two berry pickers are walking through the high mountain region. Their
names are Marie Kongsgård and Ole Grønvad. Perhaps
they are from one of the farms down in the valley. They
have been hiking for a long time, uphill the whole way,
higher and higher, because the only way to get here is to
travel by foot, and the path is long, regardless of whether
they've approached from the north, south, east, or west.

The two hikers walk out onto a large, flat bog. To the
north they can see the pastures down in the valley and farther beyond, the city of Kongsberg. To the west, where the
terrain begins rising steeply toward the mountain, beneath
the twisted dwarf birches and low, gnarled spruce trees,

they spy something unusual, something that stands out in the landscape.

If it was afternoon and the sun was already in the west, the two berry pickers would have the sun directly in their eyes as they stared toward the edge of the bog. They stop in surprise. Maybe they put their hands above their eyes to shield them from the sun.

A long boulder protrudes from the blueberry shrubs. The boulder isn't very large, perhaps three feet long and two feet wide, pale granite, soft curves at its edges. There is nothing remarkable about the boulder itself; it is what is lying on top of the boulder that has captured the berry pickers' attention.

A boy, a tiny human creature, silent and unmoving, with a cap under his head and a jacket spread out on top of him. From their vantage point it appears he might be sleeping. Or maybe they are able to see at first glance that the boy is dead.

These hikers have certainly read in the newspapers about the boy's disappearance and the search parties. Slowly, a thought begins to take shape in their minds. They approach the boulder and when they get up close, there is no longer any doubt.

The boy on the boulder is Hans Torske.

T HE SUN PEEKS OUT from behind the clouds and meets us where we are seated. Two people on top of a mountain and a sun that is gliding freely through the expanse of space. Between us and it are ninety-two million miles of black emptiness. And yet its existence is a prerequisite for all life on earth. If there were no sun up above, we would not be here down below.

August has questions, and I recount more of the story about Hans Torske.

"Not much is known about him. He only lived to be six years old, and a six-year-old who died in 1894 didn't leave much more behind than the memories of those who loved him. Those people have died too by now, and so the only thing left is a memorial plaque attached to the boulder where he was found, and a faded yellow sign that reads:

Hans Torske
Vanished July 9, 1894, on Breistulseter
Found deceased on this place on July 29, '95

"How did he die?" August asks.

I answer as best I can.

"No one knows for sure. He might have died of hunger, but that would mean he had been walking around for several days on these mountains. I don't think that's what happened, though, because then he wouldn't have been found on a boulder next to a bog that was above the farm pasture he had left. I think he died because his body temperature got too low, and that probably happened the same night that he got lost, or the next day. He walked straight up and over the steep mountain, and when he got to the top he lay down on the boulder beside the bog. Maybe it was raining, but even if the weather was nice, it can get cold at night in the mountains. If a six-year-old boy lay down to sleep, without warm clothes and with his body right up against the rock, he may have become so cold during the night that he never woke up again. If that is the way that Hans Torske died, it's somewhat comforting that he didn't have to be alone for too long."

August asks, "Where was his dad?"

I answer, "I think Hans's dad was . . ."

". . . dead? A robber? Mean? An alcoholic?"

"No, none of those things. I think that he just wasn't at the farm pasture when his son disappeared. The mother died a few years after they found her son. Some people said she died of sorrow, but I believe she died of tuberculosis, which was a common illness back then. Today the bog where Hans was found is called Torskemyra (Torske's bog) and the mountain behind the boulder where he was lying is called Torskeknatten (Torske's crag). In Kongsberg there is a little hill in the middle of the city called Torskebakken (Torske's hill). This was where Hans used to live with his family. In some archives, I've read that the dad and the older son, Erik, continued living there after Hans and his mother died. They had once been a family of six people. And only two of them were left. That's what it was like to live in Norway over a hundred years ago. A lot of people died before reaching adulthood. In the church register, where they wrote who was born and who died in Kongsberg in the 1890s, it's full of the names of children who only lived a few short years. Many of them never even lived to be as old as you are right now."

"Why didn't he find his way back?" asks August.

"Back in Hans Torske's time, they didn't know a lot about how children behave when they get lost, but we know more today. A six-year-old boy is able to walk very far, much farther than one might think. He knows when he's lost, and he wants to try to find his way back home. But his brain is a mix of practical thoughts and fantasy. He tries mostly to think about his goal, the farm that he left, and he doesn't put much thought into how best to get there. Hans Torske was too small to come up with a plan, the way that we came up with a plan for this expedition. All he could do was keep walking, on and on and on, and hope that if he walked far enough, he would finally get home."

August sits quietly. Something tells me that he is listening, so I continue.

"When a six-year-old boy gets lost, he is going to look for familiar landmarks, a mountaintop, a path, or a stream. That's one of the big differences between a six- and a seven-year-old. A seven-year-old is not only stronger and more robust, he can also understand what it means to get lost. A seven-year-old can understand the terrain and read a map. If he gets lost, he is able to remember the places he passed on the way, and this helps him find the way back. If you got lost now, you would have a much better chance of finding your way back than Hans Torske did."

August has his cap on backward and a pair of sunglasses with silver frames and blue lenses. They seem ill-placed in this context.

I say: "The saddest thing about the whole story of Hans Torske is that he was so close to his farm when he died. And that the search party had actually come very close to where he was found. In the newspaper articles I've read, it says that they searched far up the mountainside but that they turned around just before they got to the top, right where the bog is. They didn't think a small boy could have made it that far."

AUGUST STANDS and walks over to a little sign that has been screwed into the rock. He looks south. I go and stand next to him and point toward a large oval lake below.

"At the end of the lake is the black hiking hut where we started our expedition," I say. "And just beyond that is the parking lot with our car."

August stares. Between us and the car is all the terrain we've covered, the mountains and forests and all of the bodies of water gleaming in the sunlight. I turn and point to the east, toward a monotone landscape that seems endless from where we're standing. It is flat and gray and bleak. That leads, too, toward the parking lot and our car, but the distance is greater, and the trajectory is different from the one we took to get here. I explain to August that this is the way we are going to go now. I've never been this way before, but I think it is going to be nice, even if there aren't any paths.

In cases like this, August almost always reacts with unconditional enthusiasm, but not this time. He looks down at the ground. He shrugs his shoulders, turns his back to me, sits, and starts fiddling with the GPS transmitter that is attached to the top of my backpack.

Slowly it dawns on me that he does not wish to cross this barren mountain plateau. The thought of hiking even farther, maybe for days, has lost its appeal. He is tired. He misses home. He has focused all of his attention toward reaching the top of Styggemann, and in that enthusiasm to reach the top, he has forgotten that though we have achieved our goal, we still have the long journey back. There is no victory celebration to be had on top, no medals being handed out, no one to hoist us up onto their shoulders and parade us back home.

August studies the GPS transmitter with his neck bowed. I stand above him wondering what to do. In this situation, I am the autocrat and August is at the mercy of my whims. I can do whatever I feel like. I can force him to continue on the longest trajectory, or I could let it go. Maybe he would enjoy the longer route after all, maybe the last stretch would be the nicest part of the whole expedition.

Then again, maybe it wouldn't.

It's not a difficult decision. August has already covered such a long distance; this expedition has gone on for an amount of time that is almost inconceivable for such a small boy. In his memory, this hike will always be a string of indistinguishable days, both similar and different; a series of experiences both minor and monumental from this landscape the summer he was seven, experiences that he will never have again, at least not in the same way.

I say, "Let's forget about this barren mountain landscape with no paths. Let's take the shortest way back instead. What if we try to reach the car by the end of the day?"

August lets go of the GPS transmitter and lights up. From one second to the next he is transformed from a listless boy to a mountaineer who can't wait to set off. We eat until we are full and then pack our bags, and when the sun shifts from yellow to orange, we start on the long journey back to the car.

◇◇◇

I T WAS THE LIGHTEST DAY of the summer, a turning point in the endless cycle of beginnings and endings that we call a year.

We didn't stop to rest that day; we continued hiking all afternoon and evening and even after nightfall. August floated over the bogs. I followed along behind as well as I could, numb in my back and shoulders. I called out from fear that I would lose sight of him. In a moment of sheer overconfidence, he darted straight toward a dark bog hole. This made me angry. I spoke sharply to him, and afterward I had to explain that holes like that can be bottomless, and that I wasn't angry as he thought I was but rather afraid that something could happen to him.

As soon as the sun went down behind the mountains in the east, the landscape grew grim and trollish. Where earlier the air had smelled of mountain and grass and trees, it now reeked of earth and bog. The air had the chill of early summer. It was biting and intense, with an aroma so sharp it was almost a flavor. Mosquitoes and midges drifted in the shelter of the grainy half-darkness. Soon they were circling around August's pale head, but the insects no longer affected him.

◇◇◇

M Y GRANDMOTHER AND GRANDFATHER lived on a remote farm next to a large lake, surrounded by swaths of forest and tall ridges. My grandfather was a farmer and lumberjack. When he worked, he could be found in either the fields or in the forest. When he had time off, he could be found either in the fields or in the forest. His entire life was lived in close quarters with nature. He knew both the work aspects of it and the parts that corresponded to leisure. He often brought me along. It was from him that I learned the names of trees and flowers and birds and animals. I learned that nature can be beautiful but also treacherous. That the ice might crack if you step on it. That a female moose can attack if you come between her and her calf. That the bogs can be bottomless. That it's easy to get lost in the woods.

I remember wet autumn days with harsh winds and rain and falling leaves, the sort of days when no one wanted to be outside and people don't usually opt for so-called outdoor recreation but when I myself longed to be outside as much as possible. It was on precisely these days that I felt something was really happening, that it was possible to come more closely in touch with nature than on sunnier days.

This sensation was most poignant for me during the seasonal transitions. These periods mark a time of upheaval between two phases in the annual cycle, changes that have occurred an infinite number of times before and that will continue to take place each year for as long as I live, and even when I am no longer alive. I remember the first bluebell that appeared on west-facing slopes in the spring, among the previous autumn's decaying leaves and the stiff, leafless boughs of deciduous trees; the ice that suddenly settled on the water—if you listened you could hear the water molecules constricting to form a hard shell on the water's surface; the summer nights so bright that it looked like someone had sifted powdered sugar onto the pine needles in the forest where I walked with my mother and grandmother on our way to the pond to fish for trout; the intense scent of spruce when my grandfather cut down a tree in midwinter, and afterward when we sat on its green branches drinking hot cocoa from a thermos; the first autumn wind that swept across the earth where we bent over to dig up plump red potatoes that would feed us throughout the winter.

I waited for these moments every year.

It was the endless return of all things.

Nothing was new, everything was the same.

This is why I never tired of it.

In hindsight, I have come to understand that this view of nature perhaps belonged to another era. It pointed back in time more than forward. My children are growing up in a world where much has changed. These days, many people live in cities or town centers, in apartments, condos, residential areas, suburbs. Fewer and fewer children grow up in close proximity to forests, mountains, or the sea. The same goes for my children. They have less access to untouched nature than I did at their age.

Modern parents take their children on organized excursions into the wild. This is what we call outdoor recreation (or, in Norway, *friluftsliv*, literally "free air life"). Families go on the proverbial Sunday hike through the forest along a gravel backroad or a well-marked path with signposts pointing the way and the distance to the goal. The goal, in Norway and other European countries at least, is most often a hut where you can purchase buns and hot chocolate and the weekend newspaper, snap a few Instagram-worthy shots, and perhaps chat with the family at the next table. There's nothing wrong with this way of visiting nature, but it is very different from the way I grew up. The Sunday family hike is a form of physical and mental recreation that is certainly both healthy and good. This activity might last for a few hours before the family returns to their cozy house. In this way, it's not unlike an outing to a café, or visiting the swim hall, or going for a jog in the park. It is a way of being outdoors that imparts to children that nature is primarily a safe, comfortable place where, in the worst case, one may get a little tired and wet, but where it's fairly simple to return quickly to the warm safety of one's own home.

The minds of us modern parents are awash in ideals that we hope to someday realize. We would like our children to grow up more freely than any other generation, to develop a boundless confidence in their own abilities and uniqueness. Humility is the most reprehensible trait imaginable, while the appeal of unrestricted individual freedom feels to us like the very light of heaven. Still, I can't quite kick the nagging thought that maybe there is value in the opposite approach, namely that one's own greatness lies not in our individuality, but in our relationship to everything around us.

When the children were smaller, I used to bend over backward to secure opportunities for them to develop under conditions that were so tolerant and inclusive and optimally curated that they might be able to grow into unique beings in a sea of mediocrity. After a while, I grew bored. I stopped believing not in the children but in the dream that they were going to become something special. The only thing that has remained is my desire to introduce them to nature, because I believe that nature can impart some valuable experiences that will be beneficial throughout their lives. If they end up moving to Tokyo and running a nightly billiard parlor in a rundown basement, so be it. But I realized that, for my own sake, I have to give them the chance to become familiar with the natural world and to perhaps grow to love it, if you can use a word like that about something that definitely is not going to return the sentiment.

This is what it means to be in nature with children, from my perspective. I don't care about the athletic aspects: the outstanding feats, the urge to be the fastest or climb the highest. It seems to me that children get enough of these kinds of activities in their urban lives, and they can continue to tone their muscles by jumping on trampolines or balancing on curbs. But it is something else entirely to feel the timelessness that sometimes comes over you when you find yourself in a vast, wild landscape. It puts you in your place, in a sense, and it reveals something about the bigger context of which you are a small part. I don't think it's possible to have that feeling anywhere other than in nature. And because it has become increasingly important to me, I have decided that it is also important for me to share this feeling with my children.

But how is one to do this?

I don't recall anyone ever saying to me as a child: "Look at the moon! Doesn't it make you think about how small you really are?"

That's not the way to do it. But I was part of a community that held, as a basic, underlying principle, that the wild had its own intrinsic value, and that it was worth experiencing, perhaps even important or vital to do so.

Animals, birds, insects, fish, flowers, trees.

In the mountains.

In the woods.

At the coast.

Spring, summer, fall, winter.

Nature is not good. It is indifferent, it is beyond our moral constructs. It is blameless, in the way that a small child is blameless. If a small boy gets lost and dies alone in a barren wilderness high in the mountains, it's no good chastising the forest or the mountain or the bog. There is no malice in such a situation, no will behind what has occurred. It is this indifference, the non-humanness of the wild, that draws us to it. But this is also what we most fear.

You cannot bargain with a storm or convince a raging river to calm down. You cannot ask the freezing temperatures to please warm up a bit or the rain to consider stopping.

Nature has a thousand methods for taking your life. A tumble. A rockslide. A bottomless bog. Ice that splits open underfoot. Falling trees.

Nature does not care.

Not even if you are a six-year-old boy in shorts and no shoes who has recently celebrated your birthday.

◇◇◇

W<small>E HAD BEEN WALKING</small> for several hours, but there was still a long way to go. The day grew darker and with the darkness came the mist. It hovered above the black water and gave a feeling of enchantment to the air. Everyone should go into the wild on a summer twilight. It is one of the finest experiences in the world.

August reluctantly agreed to take a break.

We ate nuts and crispbread and drank water that tasted like bog.

And then we kept walking.

August placed rocks on top of every cairn he passed, a gesture of pure, blissful joy and generosity; here was a boy who did not tear down and destroy but rather built up. It wasn't until we caught a glimpse of the big lake far off that I realized I had reached the end of my strength. I was the cross-country skier now. I had surpassed the limit of what I could possibly achieve.

It was nighttime. We had been hiking since the morning, perhaps for as long as fourteen hours straight.

I asked August if we could set up the tent and walk the final distance in the morning, but my request was denied. I asked if we could take another break, but that request was also unacceptable. August continued to walk. He hardly seemed to notice the passing terrain. His thoughts were on Mama and his sister, Helena; on the cat; on his bedroom; on his favorite soccer club, Liverpool FC; on his toys and his friends at home.

◇◇◇

WHAT HAPPENED TO HANS TORSKE between the time of his disappearance on July 8, 1894, and when he was found on July 29, 1895, over one year later? For how long did he wander around on Skrim before he was unable to go another step? Was it a matter of days? Weeks?

What were his thoughts? Did he understand what had happened? Did he comprehend his own fate, or was he like an animal, walking until he could go no farther and then lying down to rest?

There are no definitive answers to these questions, but I've spoken with people who work in rescue operations, and the answers they have given me are somewhat comforting:

He lay down on the boulder because he was tired.

He wanted to rest.

He hoped, by doing so, to renew his energy.

He did not realize that he was going to die.

His body lay there throughout the summer, enveloped by green trees and white bog wool and insects flickering like gold at dusk. Soon it was autumn. The leaves changed color. Clear, cold raindrops fell onto his cheeks. The season gave way to winter. The first frosty nights. A thin layer of hoarfrost coated the boy's tiny body and the wind ruffled his hair. And the snow. Soon it covered the boy, the boulder, the bog, the mountain range.

◇◇◇

EXPERIMENTED WITH CARRYING MY BACKPACK a number of different ways to ease the pain. I leaned forward and then backward, to the left and to the right, stuck my thumbs under the shoulder straps, pressed the palms of my hands on my lower back. My muscles were utterly sapped of energy, my tendons ached; nothing helped. Just when I thought I couldn't take it any longer, the black buildings appeared at the end of the large lake where we had seen the chaffinch at the start of our expedition. We passed the buildings. I turned to look back at Styggemann for the final time.

In the middle of the gravel road close to where the car was parked was a bollard. When we first set off on our expedition, August had said to me: "When we get to this post, I'll know we're back."

The bollard came into view at the end of the road.

August ran toward it, and I didn't protest.

I watched him vanish like a breeze up along the gravel road. He no longer remembered his exhaustion. His gaze was fixed on what was directly ahead of him, as it often is with children his age. They are compelled onward; almost their entire lives are stretched out before them, and we, their parents, make up only a small part. They are with us for a short number of years before they will venture out into the great wide world. We do what we can to equip them for this life, but we cannot hold them back. At some point in time it is our task to let them go, and this thought is hard to swallow.

I trudged the remaining distance along the gravel road. I began to consider that something in us had changed, and I hoped August would come to remember this expedition and that it would mean something to him even when I was no longer here.

August passed the bollard and dropped out of sight around the bend where the car was parked. I followed slowly, feeling decrepit beneath the weight of my heavy burden. I dug the car keys out of the lid of my backpack and thought: maybe our children are the only people we can ever really know.

For the short while that we have them.

ABOUT THE WORK
ON THIS BOOK

THE DISAPPEARANCE OF HANS TORSKE drew widespread national attention when it first happened. And yet the documentation was sparse. I have read the few written sources that I was able to unearth, most of them newspaper articles describing the event, some of them at the time of the occurrence and many of them years later. I have read what I was able to dig up on the local historical literature from our own times. These are full of descriptions of Hans Torske's disappearance, but all of them are short and incomplete and so similar that it seems they have used each other as sources. The bar for precision is low.

Only a few weeks after his disappearance, various theories began to arise as to why Hans Torske disappeared and when he was last seen, and what he did then. Later rumors held that he was kidnapped by drifters or carried off by a bear. The same confusion circulates about the spot where he was found. I have stuck to the theory that he was indeed found on the boulder where the memorial plaque is now located, even if some sources claim that he was discovered on a low mountain slope nearby.

The choice of words and the tone of some of the narratives read more like fairy tales than historical accounts.

And perhaps this is the status that Hans Torske's story has acquired. It has become a folktale, circulated primarily by word of mouth, passed on from generation to generation, because there is something gripping and universal about it and also because it warns about just how unsparing and dangerous the wilderness can be.

Hans Torske lost his way in the woods over one hundred years ago. No one who was alive then is still alive now. I have spoken with people in the Kongsberg area. They have given me valuable information, but even though many of them are well on in years, they too first heard this information from their parents and grandparents.

I searched in the National Archives and the National Library digital archives for details about the original event, and also for biographical information about Hans Torske and his parents, Haagen Torske and Henriette Petrine. There was nothing whatsoever about Hans, besides a few handwritten notes in a church book after his body was found.

It is easy to get caught up in the facts when delving into old archives. At some point, I realized I would never find enough information to reconstruct this story in its entirety. Besides, it was not so much the facts of Hans Torske's story as it was his universal fate that interested me.

My descriptions of the boy in the landscape are based on what I have been able to glean from information about the weather conditions, the terrain, period clothing, and the typical behavior of children in such situations. I have hiked the distance between Breistul pasture where the farms were located and the Styggemann summit on Skrim, and I have stood at the edge of the bog next to the boulder where he was found. My descriptions of the terrain through which he passed is based on firsthand empirical data; however, my reflections around what might have happened to him along the way, how he might have walked, or what he might have thought about are purely fictional, derived from my own ideas and theories.

ORAL SOURCES

I AM GRATEFUL TO Åse Malmanger, who not only imparted her knowledge about the Hans Torske story but who also tipped me off about local historical books and put me in touch with others around Kongsberg who knew, or might have known, something about the case. Thanks also to Magne Lindtvedt and Jon Kjørstad for valuable information about the Breistul alpine pasture area; about the summer farms in the old days, the wildlife, and weather conditions on Skrim; and about the terrain where Hans Torske was last spotted. Thank you to chief medical officer Stephen Sollid with the Norwegian Air Ambulance, who contributed his knowledge and experiences to my attempt to reconstruct what might have happened to Hans Torske after he vanished, and what might have contributed in the end to his death. Thank you to climate researcher Elin Lundstad at the Norwegian Meteorological Institute, who helped me locate information pertaining to the weather conditions during the days surrounding Hans Torske's disappearance.

GRATITUDE

THANK YOU TO my Norwegian editor Sverre, for good reading and priceless support throughout this project. To Tarje, for seeing dramatic solutions long before I saw them myself. To Trude, for a sharp eye and a wise reading of the manuscript, and to both her and Helena for allowing us to set off on our expedition and for receiving us when we returned home. And finally, but also first and foremost: thank you, August, for joining me.

WRITTEN SOURCES

"Det store altet" (tr. "The Great World"). Conversation between Per Bjørn Foros and the philosophy professor Arne Johan Vetlesen. Published in *Klassekampen* on September 17, 2016.

Emerson, Ralph Waldo. "Nature." Essay taken from *Essays and Poems by Ralph Waldo Emerson*. Barnes & Noble Classics, 2004.

Eriksen, Andreas. "Hansemann i Skrim" (tr. "Hansemann in Skrim"), *Telemark Arbeiderblad*. August 20, 1950.

Forvaltningsplan for Skrim og Sauheradfjella Naturreservat (tr. *Management Plan for Skrim and Sauherad Mountain Nature Preserve*). County Commissioner in Telemark and County Commissioner in Buskerud, 2011.

Hamre, Honoria Bjerknes. *Fjellet. Fora, fauna, geologi* (tr. *The Mountain: Flora, Fauna, Geology*). Cappelen Damm, 2006.

Helleberg, Odd Arne and Dag Kristoffersen, eds. *Langs Lågen. Årbok for 2016* (tr. *Along the River: Yearbook for 2016*). Forlaget Langs Lågen, 2016.

Koester, Robert J. *Lost Person Behavior*. dbS Productions, 2008.

Langs Lågen. Natur og kultur fra Larvik til vidda (tr. *Along the River: Nature and Culture from Larvik to the Plateaus*). Forlaget for historie. Langs Lågen, 1992.

Louv, Richard. *The Last Child in the Woods*. Atlantic Books, 2010.

MacKinnon, J.B. "Falsk idyll" (tr. "False Idyll"). Essay published in the online magazine *Harvest* on January 5, 2017.

Næss, Gerd. *Fjellviddens offer* (tr. *Casualty of the High Mountain*). This account is repeated in several books, among them *Langs Lågen* (tr. *Along the River*), 1992 (see above).

Såtvedt, Olav. *Skrim*. Skrim Forlag, 2012.

Solnit, Rebecca. *A Field Guide to Getting Lost*. Canongate Books, 2006.

Sulebak, Jan R. *Landformer og prosesser* (tr. *Land Formations and Processes*). Fagbokforlaget, 2007.

Sundt, Henrik. *I kong Ravals rike* (tr. *In King Raval's Kingdom*). Andresen & Butenschøn, 2008.

Tordsson, Bjørn. "Langsommere, dypere, mykere" (tr. "Slower, Deeper, Softer"). Essay published in the online magazine *Harvest* on February 24, 2016.

Trekking Association of Drammen and Opland. *Årbok 1967* (tr. *Yearbook 1967*). Harald Lyche & Co., 1967.

The song August sings on p. 50 is a tune composed for a poem by Inger Hagerup, called "Sommerøya" (tr. "The Summer Island"). The melody was composed by Finn Kalvik.

The quote from John Muir on p. 72 was taken from the book *My First Summer in the Sierras*. Canongate Books, 2014.

The quote from the hobbit Sam on p. 19 was taken from the film *The Lord of the Rings: The Fellowship of the Rings*, based on J.R.R. Tolkien's book by the same name, first published in 1954.

ALSO BY TORBJØRN EKELUND

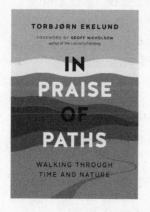

In Praise of Paths:
Walking Through Time and Nature
Available in print, ebook, and audiobook

An ode to paths and the
journeys we take through nature.

TORBJØRN EKELUND STARTED to walk—everywhere—after an epilepsy diagnosis affected his ability to drive. The more he ventured out, the more he came to love the act of walking, and an interest in paths emerged. In this poignant, meandering book, Ekelund interweaves the literature and history of paths with his own stories from the trail. As he walks with shoes on and barefoot, through forest creeks and across urban streets, he contemplates the early tracks made by ancient snails and traces the wanderings of Romantic poets, among other musings. If we still "understand ourselves in relation to the landscape," Ekelund asks, then what do we lose in an era of car travel and navigation apps? And what will we gain from taking to paths once again?

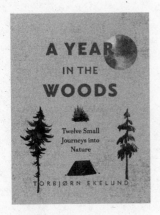

A Year in the Woods:
Twelve Small Journeys into Nature
Available in print, ebook, and audiobook

A humorous and modest
Walden *for modern times.*

TORBJØRN EKELUND WANTS to spend more time in nature, so he hatches a plan to leave the city after work one day per month, camp near the same tiny pond in the forest, and return to work the next day. He will keep up these modest journeys for a year. Evoking Henry David Thoreau and the four-season structure of *Walden*, Ekelund reflects on the quiet beauty of changing light, the thoughts of birds and fish, the unpleasantness of camping in the cold, and the banality of seeing the same sights over and over. *A Year in the Woods* asks us to reconsider our relationship with the natural world. Are we anxious wanderers or mindful observers? Do we honor the seasons or let them pass us by? And how can even the most modest of journeys enhance our lives?